T0194486

Words without Knowledge

Where Have All the Christians Gone?

Steve MacFarland

WESTBOW
PRESS®
A DIVISION OF THOMAS NELSON
& ZONDERVAN

WestBow Press books may be ordered through booksellers or by contacting:

WestBow Press
A Division of Thomas Nelson & Zondervan
1663 Liberty Drive
Bloomington, IN 47403
www.westbowpress.com
1 (866) 928-1240

ISBN: 9781-9736-2485-1(sc)
ISBN: 978-1-9736-2484-4 (hc)
ISBN: 978-1-9736-2486-8 (e)

Library of Congress Control Number: 2018905267

Print information available on the last page.

WestBow Press rev. date: 06/05/2018

It is with love and the deepest appreciation that I dedicate this book to the one who has given me the free gift of eternal life. I speak of course of the Lord Jesus Christ who, by His great grace, has forgiven me of all my sin, answered my prayers, and blessed our family abundantly through all kinds of life situations. Thank You, Jesus. Your truth has set me free, and I will be forever grateful.

Many thanks to my dear wife, Fran, who was used by the Lord to encourage me in the writing of this book and who has faithfully supported and assisted me in the ministry of Bible teaching for more than forty years. Thanks also to my good friend, Pam Hurff, who loves God's Word and kindly volunteered her editorial assistance for this project.

CONTENTS

CHAPTER 1

Introduction to the Problem

Far too many genuine Christians do not fully realize the spiritual benefits they possess, so it is easy for the slick salesmen of America's educational establishment and the promoters of our secular society to take advantage. It's like an older, self-centered brother offering to trade five shiny new fifty-cent pieces for a dirty 1918 silver dollar that his little brother found while digging in the backyard. Not realizing its value, the little brother makes the trade. Similarly, there are many Christians being taken by those who would subvert their faith in the truth of Scripture. Christians are ridiculed as living in the past, ignorant of scientific scholarship, and foolishly trusting in some antiquated, error-filled book written by men. According to several reliable studies by both Christian and secular organizations, many of America's youth who profess to be believers are leaving their Christian heritage, never to return. They have grown up in Christian families, attended Christian churches, and often attended Christian elementary and secondary schools.

The description of this crisis in America and the decline of church attendance and Christian influence in our country is documented in a book written by John S. Dickerson entitled *The Great Evangelical Recession*, published by Baker Books in 2013. In it, Dickerson states, "Research indicates that more than half of those born into evangelicalism are leaving the movement during their twenties. And the majority of them never return. This departure figure has never been higher in the United States. The number of those who return has never been lower."[1]

Furthermore, he reports that separate studies conducted by Josh McDowell, the Barna Group, Life Way Research, and secular organizations such as UCLA found that up to 80 percent of evangelicals in their twenties leave their Christian heritage.[2] Back in 2006, McDowell, a well-known Christian author, reported that 69 percent of evangelical teenagers do not attend church after leaving high school.[3] Is this mass exodus occurring because teens really do not know the truth as found in Christ, or is in part because they have not been grounded in the truth?

It has often been said that knowledge is everything, but knowledge must be a knowledge of truth. There is something all believers need to know but few really seem to understand, and that is the nature of truth. If we were more diligent to search the Scriptures and teach our youth who profess to know Christ the nature of God's truth, I believe far fewer would stray from their Christian foundation. This book discusses what God says regarding truth and its counterparts: knowledge, wisdom, and understanding. To reap the greatest benefit from reading this book, please take the time to read the supporting passages in the Scriptures.

It is clear from internal evidence that the book of Job was probably the first book of the Bible to be written. Those who are familiar with the account may remember that God challenged Satan regarding the righteous character of His servant, Job, who feared God and hated evil. Satan took up the challenge, claiming that Job worshipped God only because He was protecting him and had greatly blessed him. In other words, Job was just using God for what he could get in return; his motive was not pure. Job is described as the wealthiest of all who lived in the east.

Satan's response to God was, "Take away all the blessings and Job will curse you."

So though Job was a righteous man, God permitted Satan to bring disaster down on his life. He lost his great wealth. His ten children were killed in a storm. He lost his health. He lost it all, except his wife and a few friends. Satan no doubt spared them because he planned to use them to verbally attack Job. His wife urged him to curse God (Job 2:7–10), and his friends repeatedly accused him of sin, explaining that Job's suffering was God's judgment on him and that he actually had received less punishment than he deserved (Job 11:1–6).

The central section of the book, chapters 4–31, is a discourse in which three of his friends, Eliphaz, Bildad, and Zophar, repeatedly but unsuccessfully attempted to attack Job's character. Finally, in Job 32:1–12, Elihu, the youngest, spoke for the first time. He had been quiet up until then, deferring to those who were older and supposedly wiser than he. When their arguments were exhausted, he spoke, accusing his elders of condemning Job without proof and criticizing him for justifying himself rather than God. Job could not see beyond this earthly scene to realize what was going on between God and Satan. He had no understanding of any of God's ultimate purposes in allowing Satan to test him, and if God had not revealed them to us, we would never know them either. Clearly, Job didn't know at the time that he was a test case to glorify God and to teach us great spiritual lessons about suffering.

In Elihu's criticism and rebuke of Job, he twice pointed out, in Job 34:35 and in 35:16, that in all of Job's verbose complaints about how unfair his suffering had been, he had spoken words without wisdom and knowledge. Elihu was absolutely right. How do we know? First of all, according to Job 42:7–9, when God corrected Job's three friends for their condemning criticism and ordered them to go to Job and offer up sacrifices for their sin, He issued no words of correction to Elihu. Second, when God finally broke His silence with that famous list of seventy questions in chapters 38–41, the first thing God said was that Job had been speaking words without knowledge. In other words, "Job, you don't know what you're talking about." Third, when Job spoke in 42:1–6, he agreed with God that he had spoken words without understanding.

We can't find fault with Job for not knowing what was going on. How could he know unless God revealed it to him? Elihu's argument was that Job's focus was on his innocence of anything worthy of such suffering rather than on his sovereign God's righteousness. Job was in the process of learning the great lesson that all need to learn, and that is, in spite of what our Western culture teaches us, life is not all about us. It's all about God. Job wanted his day in court to plead his case with God, but when that day came in chapter 40, he put his hand over his mouth and didn't want to say a thing. The book of Job shows that God justified him in the end, restored him completely, gave him ten more children, doubled his wealth, and added 140 years to his life.

But here's the point I want you to see: Job spent a lot of time talking about things he had no knowledge of. He did not know the facts. The truth was not revealed to him until the end. **There is a type of truth that humans cannot know unless God directly reveals it, and God chooses when and how and to whom He will reveal it.** That is why unsaved people are far, far out in left field when speaking about certain things they declare to be true, when they are actually speaking words without knowledge. They do not know the truth. We will discuss this more thoroughly in the next chapter.

CHAPTER 2

What Is Truth, and Where Is It Found?

illustrated by: Brianna MacFarland

Can we define truth? Students can spend a whole semester in a secular philosophy class, exploring various historical answers and theories without coming to a final definitive conclusion. There is even a consensus theory, which teaches that truth is whatever a specific group believes is true. While not wanting to be unkind, I find such an idea to be, in the famous expression of an old Oscar Meyer commercial, "b-o-l-o-g-n-a." If it was said that Theodore

Roosevelt was president during the American Civil War, and if it were taught in every public school in America and believed by every American teenager, it still would not be true. Why? Because it does not agree with reality. **From a Christian perspective, truth is that which agrees with the reality that God has spoken, created, and sovereignly controls.**

Scripture records in John 18:37 that Jesus came into the world to bear witness to God's truth, and furthermore, that while not everyone will hear it, those who are of the truth will listen to His teaching. Pontius Pilate, the infamous Roman governor of Judea, once asked Jesus the famous question, "What is truth?" Sadly, Pilate didn't wait for an answer. He immediately turned around and left the presence of God's Son, the source of truth (John 14:6) and, without exaggeration, the one Person in all the world most capable of answering that all-important question. Had Jesus desired to answer Pilate's question, He could have done it as follows.

Scriptures clearly teach that God is the source of all truth and that He reveals it to His creation: "Lead me in Your truth and teach me, For You are the God of my salvation" (Psalm 25:5 KJV). "He shall judge the world with righteousness, And the peoples with His truth" (Psalm 96:13 NKJV). "You are near, O LORD, And all Your commandments are truth" (Psalm 119:151 NKJV). "Into Your hand I commit my spirit; You have redeemed me, O LORD God of truth" (Psalm 31:5 NKJV). "So that he who blesses himself in the land shall bless himself by the God of truth, and he who takes an oath in the land shall swear by the God of truth" (Isaiah 65:16 NKJV). Scriptures also teach that God will cut off truth from the nation that turns its back on Him: "This is a nation that does not obey the voice of the LORD their God nor receive correction. Truth has perished and has been cut off from their mouth" (Jeremiah 7:28 NKJV).

Just as God is the source of all truth in the Old Testament, His Son, Jesus Christ, who is God in the flesh, is clearly identified in the New Testament as the source of truth. He is also identified as the Creator, sustainer, and purpose of life. In addition to John 14:6 and 18:37, which were previously cited, consider the following passages:

Christ created everything that exists, which would clearly include truth (John 1:1–3).

The Word (God's Son) took on a human body and lived among us. He was full of grace and truth (John 1:14, 17).

The apostle Paul reports that truth is in Jesus (Ephesians 4:21).

Christ is the source of all that was created, whether visible or invisible, whether in heaven or on earth, and the purpose of all creation is to glorify Christ. It is by His power that all life is sustained (Colossians 1:16–17).

He is to have the preeminence in all things (Colossians 1:18). Since He is the source of truth, that surely would include education. While many in our secular culture presently deny the relevance and importance of recognizing Christ as the source of truth, Scripture tells us that "the wrath of God is revealed from heaven against all ungodliness and unrighteousness of men, who by their unrighteousness suppress the truth" (Romans 1:18 ESV). Romans 2:8 also says that God's wrath will be poured out on those who do not obey the truth.

Speaking of Christ, we are told that in Him "are hidden all the treasures of wisdom and knowledge" (Colossians 2:3 NKJV).

If God's Word is true, and I sincerely hope that with all your heart you know it is, then any society that ignores God is headed for the same serious consequences as are recorded in Psalm 9:17 and Romans 1:18–32.

Now, Christian friends, here is a question for you to consider, and I speak in generalities, for there are local exceptions. The United States has been considered by many to be the greatest nation in the history of the world. Why is it, then, that we rank so low in education compared to other major countries? Why do we presently have such a poor system of public education? It is so poor, in fact, that public educators, who are constantly crying for more money as the answer to most of our educational problems, find it necessary to spend great amounts of money on advertising, trying to convince the public that our system of education works and is getting better all the time. Could the answer to my question have anything to do with the fact that, as a nation, we have turned our back on the God of truth, who is the very source of true knowledge, wisdom, and understanding? When times of national trouble, terror, pain, or suffering occur, our leaders call for a moment of useless silence or even a time of prayer. In practice, however, we declare that the God whose help was sought at the founding of our nation now has no place in our public classrooms. We claim to be "one nation under God," but we are like those described in the book of Matthew: "This people honors me with their lips but their heart is far from Me" (Matthew 15:8 ESV). How foolish of us to forsake the God who gave us our national freedoms. How foolish of us as a nation to think that He will help us in time of trouble when we treat His words with gross disrespect. If He does help us, it will only be due to His great grace, mercy, and patience, and not because we truly honor Him.

Getting back to my original subject, it is commonly recognized that there are two general types of truth. One might be called **objective** or **absolute** and the other **subjective** or **relative**. Objective truth is absolute fact, while subjective truth is dependent on an individual's personal opinion. Some may believe that peas are little green balls of mush that have a disgusting taste, while chocolate cheesecake is positively delicious. Others may argue that such a statement, based on their opinion and personal experience, is not true. Though I believe the statement is true, I would have to admit that it is only my subjective truth and not objective truth. To illustrate again, many believe that Christmas is the best day of the year, but if you lost someone you loved due to a tragic car accident on Christmas Day, you might change your opinion regarding that subjective statement.

That America was the first to land a man on the moon, or that anyone who jumps from a fourth-floor balcony will go down and not up, are examples of objective truth. Whether or not a person believes objective truth does not change the reality of that truth. Even if a million people from New York City are certain that they are capable of swimming all the way to England on a cold day in January, the objective truth, based upon God's laws of nature, states that not one would come even remotely close to being successful in such a venture.

Now within the category of objective truth, there are two

types. (Listen, Christian, this is crucial for you to understand.) One type theologians have labeled **natural revelation** (sometimes called general revelation). Natural revelation is truth that God reveals to His created beings through the physical world. It is truth that is found in nature. The other type, which is by far the more important type, could be called **supernatural revelation** (or special revelation).

The very nature of the word *revelation* indicates that something is hidden and must in some way be discovered, uncovered, found, or realized. God has designed the truth of natural revelation, truth placed by Him in the natural world, to be discovered by humankind using the five senses and the reasoning ability we were created with. It is said that Euclid, the famous Greek mathematician known as the father of geometry, discovered mathematical relationships. He did not create them. God created them and designed humans with the ability to find them.

Supernatural revelation, on the other hand, cannot be discovered merely with the five senses and human reasoning. Something more is needed, something humans do not naturally possess by virtue of their creation. That is why it is called supernatural. Something beyond our ability is needed to discover this type of truth. What information is contained within this type of truth, and how can we obtain it if it is beyond our natural ability?

Supernatural revelation includes, among other things, the answers to the following extremely important questions:

1. How can God be known?
2. Who is He, and what is His character?
3. What are His works i.e., what does He do?

11

4. What is His relationship to humanity?
5. What are His plans for the future?

Based on the teaching of such biblical passages as Romans 1–2, Psalm 19:1, and Psalm 97:6, the fact that there is a God would be considered natural revelation. Humans were created with an innate knowledge of God, and nature shows His existence. Scripture also teaches us that we were created with a sense of morality. As Paul wrote to the church of Rome, humans have a sense of God's law written in their hearts. Though we have a sense of right and wrong, it is distorted by sin; according to Scripture, our conscience may be weak, defiled, or hardened by sin. Again, humans innately believe in a divine power and possess a moral compass. This is true of every ancient people group that has been discovered and every group that exists in the world today. While it is true that atheists may have the sense of God educated out of them by parents or an anti-God culture, they are not born that way.

Additionally, included within supernatural revelation are the answers to the following age-old philosophical questions:

1. What is the meaning of life?
2. What is the origin of humans?
3. What is the nature of humans?
4. Why do humans exist, and what is our purpose in life?
5. Where are we going?
6. How should we live?
7. What should we value in life, and why?

While humans, searching for answers throughout the centuries, have gone to Eastern and Western philosophers, gurus on mountaintops, and famous oracles, in the modern world, we simply Google it. But what answers do we find? The answer is, everything imaginable, including there are no answers. Which answer, if any, is correct?

My purpose in writing this book is to reach out to true Christians who have repented of sin, put their faith in Jesus Christ, and are saved by God's grace alone, to help them better understand one of the amazing blessings that our great God has given to His children. Being armed with that knowledge and putting it into practice, they will have the help they need to live wisely in this corrupt and sin-cursed world. If you are one of God's children through faith in Christ, then as you read over those two lists of questions, perhaps you were thinking to yourself, *I know the answer to most [or all] of these questions.* My question to you now is, "How did you become so smart when the vast majority of people in the world, including many who may be far more intelligent, have no idea what the correct answers are?" Their answers are full of words without knowledge.

Actually, these truths have little to do with intelligence but much to do with wisdom. "The fear of the LORD is the beginning of wisdom, and knowledge of the Holy One is insight" (Proverbs 9:10 ESV). As you consider your answers, and if they are correct, you will immediately realize that all of the answers are found in God's Word. In the Bible, God reveals to believers all of the life-saving, life-changing, life-guiding truths that humankind needs to know to live a life that is complete, productive, and beneficial, both for this life and for eternity. Such a life is filled with love, joy, inner peace, security, and the endless blessing of our heavenly Father. "Your word is a lamp to my feet and a light to my path" (Psalm 119:105 ESV). The apostle Paul said, when writing to the church of Ephesus, "I do not cease to give thanks for you, remembering you in my prayers, that the God of our Lord Jesus Christ, the Father of glory, may give you the Spirit of wisdom and of revelation in the knowledge of him, having the eyes of your hearts enlightened, that you may know what is the hope to which he has called you, what are the riches of his glorious inheritance in the saints, and what is the immeasurable greatness of his power toward us who believe" (Ephesians 1:16–19 ESV). Please note that this knowledge from God (supernatural revelation) is a gift that He gives to believers.

CHAPTER 3

How Do Believers Obtain Supernatural Revelation?

As for the questions of how we can obtain this truth if it is beyond our natural ability, and how supernatural revelation is learned, let me first demonstrate with a vivid illustration from Scripture, showing in chronological order the four recorded occasions when Christ was preparing His disciples for the crucifixion and resurrection.

First, a brief introduction: It is clear that early on, the disciples had a very limited understanding of who Jesus was. This becomes obvious with a careful reading of the gospels. In Mark 4, we read of the time when Jesus and the disciples are in a storm in the Sea of Galilee. He is sleeping in the stern of the boat while they were probably frenetically bailing, for the waves were washing in, and these seasoned fishermen were terrified, thinking that they would all be drowned. They woke up Jesus and asked Him if He cared that they were about to die. Jesus got up and told the wind and waves to be quiet, and the disciples were dumbfounded.

They exclaimed, "Who can this be, that even the wind and the sea obey Him!" (Mark 4:41 NKJV). Surely at this point, they had no understanding that the teacher they followed was the God of creation.

Then Jesus used the disciples to feed a hungry crowd of five thousand men, plus women and children, using five loaves of bread and two fish. The disciples gathered up twelve baskets full of all the leftovers. That evening, according to the account given in Mark 6, Jesus sent the disciples across the Sea of Galilee to Bethsaida. You are probably very familiar with the event. It is the time when a storm blew up, and in the fourth watch of the night, somewhere between 4 and 6 a.m., they saw Jesus walking on the water. Being terrified, for they thought they saw a ghost, they cried out, but the Lord quickly identified Himself and told them not to be afraid. "Then He went up into the boat to them, and the wind ceased. And they were greatly amazed in themselves beyond measure, and marveled. For they had not understood about the loaves, because their heart was hardened" (Mark 6:51–52 NKJV).

Now, Christian friend, if you saw Jesus walk on water today, would you respond the same way that the disciples did? I don't think so. Why? Because you know that He is God incarnate; however, they were still on what we might call a learning curve. Note that they were shocked because they didn't understand what the miracle of the loaves demonstrated about His nature. Could He have used one loaf of bread and a tail fin? How about a bread crumb and a fish scale? Could He have used nothing? Oh, wait; He already did that when He created the world by simply speaking.

Next, in Mark 8, we read that Jesus used the disciples to feed a great crowd that had been following Him for three days. This time, they had seven loaves and a few fish to feed four thousand men, plus women and children. When everyone was well satisfied, the disciples filled seven large baskets full of the leftovers. Shortly after that, He again set off in a boat with the disciples, and Mark makes a point of telling us that they had only taken one loaf of bread with them. According to Matthew 16, when they reached their destination, Jesus warned them to watch out for the leaven of the Pharisees and Sadducees. The disciples thought Jesus was concerned because of their small bread supply.

It almost seems comical when you think about it; especially when you consider the many thousands He recently fed using just a few loaves and a few fish. Why would the Master be concerned with their shortage of bread? But Jesus was not laughing. In fact, He seemed quite frustrated with their lack of spiritual perception.

He said to them, "Why do you reason because you have no bread? Do you not yet perceive nor understand? Is your heart still hardened? Having eyes, do you not see? And having ears, do you not hear? And do you not remember?" (Mark 8:17–18 NKJV).

This is the second time that Jesus has commented about the condition of their heart. It is extremely important for us to realize that our ability to understand the Lord's teaching (i.e., supernatural revelation) is directly connected to the state of the human heart.

The writer of Hebrews has this to say about the cause of a hardened heart: "Take heed, brethren, lest there be in any of you an evil heart of unbelief, in departing from the living God. But exhort one another daily, while it is called Today; lest any of you be hardened through the deceitfulness of sin" (Hebrews 3:12–13 KJV).

Jesus then continued, "How is it you don't understand that I was not talking to you about bread? But be on your guard against the yeast of the Pharisees and Sadducees" (Matthew 16:11 NIV). Now the disciples get it. They finally perceive the meaning of the Lord's warning. For the Scriptures go on to say, "Then they understood that he was not telling them to guard against the yeast used in bread, but against the teaching of the Pharisees and Sadducees" (Matthew 16:12 NIV). Question: If Jesus was walking in human form among us today, do you think He would tell us to avoid any particular teaching? Would He warn us about listening to those who do not have a personal knowledge of God in their hearts when they speak about issues that require that knowledge?

Now let us consider and evaluate, in chronological order, the occasions during which Jesus prepared the disciples for the crucifixion. Following the feeding of five thousand in Matthew 14 and then the feeding of four thousand in Matthew 15, Jesus asked the twelve disciples who people thought He was. They replied that some believed He was the resurrected John the Baptist, who had recently been murdered by Herod the tetrarch. Others thought He was the prophet Elijah or Jeremiah, returned to earth. Having observed great miracles on many occasions, they believed that Jesus must be some great prophet empowered by God.

Then Jesus turned to the twelve disciples and asked them the same question: "Who do you think I am?"

Peter spoke up with this answer: "You are the Christ [the Messiah], the Son of the living God" (Matthew 16:16 ESV). Peter's understanding of who Jesus is has significantly increased. Jesus then told Peter that he had been blessed by God, for it was God who had revealed this truth to him. He could not have learned it on his own. The identity of Jesus the Messiah would be impossible for humans to know. It would have to be supernaturally revealed by God.

Peter must have been elated. Not only did he get the test question right, the Master had said that he had been given divine revelation and was blessed by God. Awesome! Peter's elation was short-lived, however, because Jesus would soon rebuke him, and this is what I want you to see. Matthew records that just after Peter declared what God the Father revealed to him, Jesus began to prepare the twelve for His departure from the world. He told them for the **first time** that "He must go to Jerusalem and suffer many things from the elders and chief priests and scribes, and be killed, and on the third day be raised" (Matthew 16:21 ESV).

What Jesus said seems crystal clear. In fact, Mark 8:32 tells us that Jesus spoke this plainly or openly to them. Dear Christian, I'm sure you understand what Jesus revealed, and you believe it, don't you? Do you believe it because you understand it, or do you understand it because you believe it? Ponder that for a moment, and then notice Peter's response in Matthew 16:22: He took Jesus aside, perhaps out of earshot of the others, and with a rebuke, corrected Him, saying that God the Father would never let it happen.

Clearly, Peter did not believe what Jesus told him. Did Peter understand? Well, yes and no. We might say that he understood the words on some superficial level, but he didn't really understand. Peter could not reconcile what Jesus said with what he knew the prophets had said regarding the coming of a Messiah who would ascend the throne of David, restore the kingdom that Israel once possessed, and reign in righteousness forever. Had he truly understood, he never would have corrected the one he had just, by God's revelation, called "the Son of the living God."

Jesus then rebuked Peter by saying, "Get behind me, Satan! You are a stumbling block to me; you do not have in mind the concerns of God, but merely human concerns" (Matthew 16:23 ESV). So much for Peter's elation. By the way, Christian, here is a question for each of us to consider: Are our minds occupied with the things that concern our Lord, or are we mostly focused on "merely human concerns"?

The **second time** Jesus brought up the subject of His departure from this earth was on top of the Mount of Transfiguration. In Mark 9:1, we find that Jesus had told the disciples that some of them would not die before they had seen "the kingdom of God come with power." True to His word, six days later, He selected Peter, James, and John to travel with Him up a high mountain. It was probably Mount Hermon, which is near Caesarea Philippi. There He was transfigured before them. He appeared in the dazzling brilliance that He will have when He reigns in God's kingdom. The three disciples were permitted a glimpse of His kingdom glory. Moses and Elijah also appeared, speaking with Jesus, as we learn in Luke 9:30–31, about His "departure." The Greek word is transliterated "*exodos.*" In other words, He referred to His exit from this world which, Luke records, would be fulfilled in the city of Jerusalem. In Mark 9:9–10, we find that as they descended the mountain, Jesus ordered them to keep what they had seen a secret until after His resurrection. Verse 10 tells us that they questioned each other as to what Jesus meant when He spoke about rising again. Once again, there was a lack of understanding.

On the **third occasion,** as He was traveling through Galilee heading toward Capernaum, we are told that He traveled secretly, without the crowds, because He wanted to spend time with His disciples, preparing them for what would happen to Him when they reached Jerusalem. Again Jesus told them, as recorded in Mark 9:30–32, that He would be delivered into the hands of men who would kill Him, but three days later, He would arise. However, they didn't understand Him, and Mark added that they were afraid to ask Him for an explanation. If we look at the parallel passage in Luke 9:43–45, we begin to see why they did not understand. Luke tells us that the truth Jesus spoke to them "was hidden from them."

On the **fourth and final occasion** on record, as Jesus headed to Jerusalem for the climax of His earthly life, He revealed to the twelve in even greater detail that which they were about to witness: "See, we are going up to Jerusalem, and the Son of Man will be delivered over to the chief priests and the scribes, and they will condemn Him to death and deliver Him over to the Gentiles. And they will mock Him and spit on Him, and flog Him and kill Him. And after three days he will rise" (Mark 10:33–34 ESV).

Okay, then, that should clear up any misunderstanding. He had just explained to them for the fourth time and in the greatest detail what was about to take place. And you, my Christian friend, certainly understand what Jesus told them. He could not have been more clear. So why is it that you understand, but they did not? Luke 18:34 tells us that they didn't understand a thing He said. If you look up the verse, you'll notice that it goes on to say that the truths Jesus had just given to them **were hidden from them** so that they couldn't understand.

Now here is your first question: Was Jesus telling them subjective or objective truth? If you answered objective, you are thinking logically. If you said subjective, you may need to go back and read the first chapter of this book again. Now, I'll ask question number two: Was Jesus telling them truth we would call natural revelation, or was it supernatural revelation? Was it truth they could discover by researching in the natural world, or was it truth they could not possibly know if God did not reveal it in some supernatural way? Obviously, the answer is supernatural revelation. Now I'll ask a third question: If God's Son was revealing this to them, why didn't they understand it? The answer is found in realizing how supernatural revelation is learned and in understanding who gives the insight to comprehend it. This will be discussed in detail shortly. Remember that the Scripture said that the truth Jesus spoke was hidden from them. Therefore, we can absolutely conclude that supernatural revelation is not something that can be understood simply because it is heard or read or even seen.

I'm reminded of an Old Testament passage in which Moses spoke the following words to the Israelites after, by God's grace and power, he led them out of Egypt and through the wilderness for forty years: "You have seen all that the LORD did before your eyes in the land of Egypt, to Pharaoh and to all his servants and to all his land, the great trials that your eyes saw, the signs, and those great wonders. But to this day the LORD has not given you a heart to understand or eyes to see or ears to hear" (Deuteronomy 29:2–4 ESV).

I'm also reminded of a passage where, just prior to our Lord's return to the Father, He said to His disciples, "'These are my words that I spoke to you while I was still with you, that everything written about me in the Law of Moses and the Prophets and the Psalms must be fulfilled.' Then He opened their minds to understand the Scriptures, and said to them, 'Thus it is written, that the Christ should suffer and on the third day rise from the dead, and that repentance and forgiveness of sins should be proclaimed in his name to all nations, beginning from Jerusalem'" (Luke 24:44–47 ESV).

When God opens the minds of believers, we are blessed with the ability to understand supernaturally revealed truth. Those who walk in darkness and are deaf and blind to God's truth cannot understand supernatural revelation. However, as previously noted, passages such as Ephesians 1:15–23 tell us that God has blessed those of us who are His children by a second or spiritual birth with the gift of divine knowledge; that is, the knowledge of God, His character, His will, His purposes, and His plans for the future. In John 16:13, Jesus tells us that the Spirit will reveal to us things that will come in the future. As to how this type of truth is obtained, the Bible is quite clear. Supernatural revelation is learned by faith, and God's Spirit is the teacher with the power to enlighten us; that is, to cause us to understand. True, we need our God-given senses coupled with the ability to reason logically, but that alone is not enough. That is exactly why the unsaved mind is not capable of comprehending this most important type of truth. Once again, let me demonstrate with a clear illustration from Paul's first recorded letter to the church of Corinth and, following that, with a message from the book of Job:

Paul, reflecting on his first visit to the city of Corinth, wrote to the believers about his manner in presenting to them the gospel of Christ. He said, "And my speech and my preaching were not with persuasive words of human wisdom, but in demonstration of the Spirit and of power, that your faith should not be in the wisdom of men but in the power of God" (1 Corinthians 2:5–6 NKJV). He calls this human wisdom the "wisdom of words" in 1:17, the "wisdom of the wise" in 1:19, and the "wisdom of this world" in 1:20. Then in 1:21, Paul explained that by God's wise plan, He grants eternal life to those who put their faith in Him, but the wisdom of the world will never result in us knowing God.

This fact was also revealed to believers way back in the book of Job, which as previously stated was probably the first book of the Bible to be written. In Job 28:12, Job asked his friends where true wisdom and understanding could be found. Then in verses 13–28, he raised the following questions and answered them for us:

Question: Where is wisdom *not* found? (verses 13, 14)

Answer: In the land of the living.

Question: What is it worth? (verses 15–19)

Answer: It is beyond the value of all precious things.

Question: From whom is it hidden? (verses 20-22)

Answer: It is hidden from every living thing.

Question: Who understands and knows it? (verses 23–27)

Answer: Only God.

Question: What does God say to humankind? (verse 28)

Answer: Wisdom is fearing the Lord, and departing from evil shows understanding.

Once again, it is "the fear of the Lord"—a respect for and submission to His sovereignty, resulting in a personal relationship with Him through Jesus Christ—that is the starting point for true wisdom and knowledge. "The fear of the LORD *is* the beginning of knowledge: *but* fools despise wisdom and instruction" (Proverbs 1:7 KJV). "The fear of the LORD *is* the beginning of wisdom: and the knowledge of the holy *is* understanding" (Proverbs 9:10 KJV). (Note: for a further explanation of the fear of the Lord, please see addendum 1.) It is the true, personal knowledge of the living God that results in eternal life. As Jesus explained in the Gospel of John, "And this is eternal life, that they may know You, the only true God, and Jesus Christ whom You have sent" (John 17:3 NKJV).

God's true wisdom is set in contrast to human wisdom. Paul went on to say, "But we speak the wisdom of God in a mystery, the hidden wisdom which God ordained before the ages for our glory" (1 Corinthians 2:7 NKJV). In the next verse, Paul then pointed out that the leaders of our world would never have crucified Christ if they had only known who He was, but they didn't, and they couldn't. Paul explained this by quoting Isaiah 64:4 in 1 Corinthians 2:9 (KJV): "But as it is written, Eye hath not seen, nor ear heard, neither have entered into the heart of man, the things which God hath prepared for them that love him."

I think that last verse is probably one of the most misunderstood verses in the Bible. Many times, I've heard it quoted by someone who is saying heaven is so wonderful that it is beyond our imagination. But if you look at the following verse, 1 Corinthians 2:10, Paul expressly stated that God's plans for his children have been revealed to us by the teacher of supernatural revelation, the Holy Spirit. If you've read your Bible, and I trust you read it daily, then you know a good bit of what the kingdom of God on earth and our future in heaven will be like because this has been revealed to you by the Spirit. Verse 10 ends with the fact that the Spirit can reveal such information because He searches and knows even "the deep things of God."

What are you thinking right now? Are you deep in thought about some spiritual truth stated in the last few paragraphs? Did your mind wander over to something you have planned for tomorrow? Perhaps your mind is on food. I have no idea what you are thinking. I only know what I am thinking, and that is the point of verse 11. Only your spirit knows your thoughts, and in the same way, only God's Spirit knows what God is thinking. Now I would really like you to follow my direction on a short spiritual exercise. Please take your Bible and carefully read 1 Corinthians 2:12–14 and then answer the following questions:

1. According to verse 12, where is the Spirit of God?
2. According to verses 12–13, what is He doing there?
3. What does it cost? (How much is tuition?)

4. From verse 14, can you tell why the natural or unsaved person is not able to understand the teachings of God's Spirit? What does the unsaved person consider those teachings to be?

(The answers are at the end of this chapter, but resist the temptation to peek.)

From this illustration alone, it should be clear that there are truths that God has revealed only to the believer. There is a type of truth that theologians call special or supernatural revelation that only true believers can comprehend. This truth is called the "things of God" in 1 Corinthians chapter 2. The unsaved consider it to be foolish because that knowledge is learned through a faith that they do not possess. They just can't see it.

Another illustration is found in the book of Hebrews: "By faith we understand that the universe was formed at God's command, so that what is seen was not made out of what was visible" (Hebrews 11:3 NIV). Scripture teaches that we believe by faith that God created all that exists simply through speaking, exactly as it is recorded in Genesis 1:1–31. Evolutionists believe by faith (for there is no proof) that material has eternally existed and has evolved into its present form over billions of years. That clearly contradicts God's Word. The verse states that nothing we can see originated from anything visible. Is your faith in what the Creator says or in what the evolutionist says?

Some twenty-five hundred years ago, a man named Daniel made a decision to be faithful to the Lord, even though he had been taken captive by King Nebuchadnezzar and moved to Babylon.

You may know the account from Daniel 2:1–49, but let me point something out to you. The king had a troubling dream and called all the wise men of Babylon for help. To check on their honesty and accuracy, he demanded that they tell him both the dream and its meaning or be executed. They objected, saying it was an unfair request. No king ever made such a demand. They said it is impossible for anyone to tell him what only the gods could know, and they don't live among men. Daniel with his three friends, Hananiah, Michael, and Azariah, prayed to the one true God, who revealed the secret to Daniel in a vision. Daniel then praised his Lord, the source of wisdom and knowledge, and told the king all the details of his dream. Here is the point: Daniel agreed with the wise men. There are things which are impossible for humans to know, but Daniel's God reveals such things to believers. (For further discussion please see addendum 5.)

Answers to 1 Corinthians 2:12–14 questions:

1. God's Spirit indwells the believer.
2. He is in us to teach us the things of God.
3. These great truths are free to us.
4. These truths are spiritually learned or discerned through faith, which the unsaved do not have. That is why the unsaved consider the things of God to be foolishness.

CHAPTER 4

Those Who Are Lost Are Blind to the Things of God

a blind couple

Scriptures contain many illustrations of spiritual blindness. Let me list some of them for you to drive this vital point home and to help you understand what truths are contained within the things of God.

One of the greatest illustrations comes from Christ's teaching as He logically reasons with those who "believed" in Him, as recorded in John 8:30–59. I placed the word *believed* in quotation marks to point out the fact that the Bible plainly shows that it is possible for people to believe, yet not in the way that saves. As we sometimes say, "Some believe with the head but not the heart." Some have an intellectual knowledge of Christ, but they don't know Him personally. In the same way, the Bible shows that people can see or hear what God says but not really perceive or truly understand, as is demonstrated in John chapter 6. The reason, of course, is that according to Scripture, the unsaved person is spiritually deaf, blind, and dead. We should not expect the lost to understand supernatural revelation unless the Spirit is working in their hearts to give them faith by which to trust in Christ.

In John 8:30–31, Jesus addressed those who believed in Him, and He told them the following:

Verses 31–32: They would truly be His disciples if they continued to follow His teaching. Immediately, with the "if" clause, He gave them a test of true faith and also raised the question of whether or not they truly believed. Then in verse 32, He exclaimed that those who were His true disciples would know the truth, and the truth would free them. At this point, we should ask the following questions: What kind of truth would free them, and from what would they be free? Obviously, Jesus is pointing to supernatural revelation setting them free, not to any truth found in natural revelation. Further, the context clearly shows that He was referring to freedom from sin. What an awesome and astounding thought. Scripture tells us in Romans 6:23 that "the wages of sin is death." That is, the payment for our sin is death, eternal separation from our Creator. And all of us have sinned, according to Romans 3:23. There is, however, a truth revealed by Christ that can set humans free from sin and give them eternal life.

Verse 33: In their reply, the believers revealed that they were not thinking on the same plane. They pointed out that they were Abraham's descendants and had never been in bondage. Exactly what they meant by that is difficult to discern, since the nation of Israel had been in bondage to several other countries over the years, including Egypt, Assyria, Babylon, Persia, and Greece. At the time of writing, they were under the very heavy hand of Rome. However, perhaps they were thinking of themselves personally, alluding to the fact that they did have a certain degree of freedom permitted them by Rome, as long as they abided by Rome's dictates.

Verses 34–37: Jesus responded with a "double verily," which could be translated as "truly, truly." It was an expression used only by Christ, recorded only by the apostle John, and meant to grab the attention of the listeners because the truth that followed was extremely important. He explained that He was speaking spiritually; sin enslaves, but the Son could free them. He then explained that He knew they were descended from Abraham, but they were seeking to kill Him because His truth was not in them. As expressed in John 2:24–25, Jesus knows what is in the human heart.

Verse 38: Jesus expressed the fact that, spiritually speaking, they and He had two different fathers. He spoke what He had heard His father say, and their actions mirror what they see their father doing. No doubt, he seemed to speak in riddles. They did not understand Him, but then again, how could they? They were spiritually deaf.

Verses 39–40: They responded again with the claim that Abraham was their father. Jesus agreed with them earlier, in verse 37, but now He questioned their claim. He had not changed His mind. He was expressing that, while He knew they were physically related to father Abraham, they were not spiritually related to him. He was not their spiritual father because, as Jesus pointed out, they were not acting like Abraham acted. He explained this concept further in verse 40. These who believed in Him desired to kill the one who had spoken God's truth to them, and that was not something father Abraham would have done. If they had the same faith that Abraham had, they would have lived and walked by faith in the living God, as Abraham did (Hebrews 11:8–10, 17–19). It was another example of the old adages, "The apple doesn't fall far from the tree" and "He's a chip off the old block."

Verses 41–43: Again, Jesus stated they were acting like their father. They replied that God was their father. Jesus had not named their father yet, but He challenged their claim by stating that if God really was their father, they would have loved Jesus, for Jesus came from God. Now, please look carefully at verse 43. Here, our Lord clearly explained why they didn't understand His teaching and why they couldn't understand supernatural revelation. **They couldn't hear Him**. It was not just that they didn't listen, like some distracted husband who's not listening to his wife, but that they were not capable of hearing His teaching due to the type of truth He spoke, as further explained in verse 45.

Verse 44: Jesus here made what might be considered a controversial and shocking statement. It is shocking, yes, but it is only controversial to those who do not understand. He said, "You belong to your father, the devil, and you want to carry out your father's desires. He was a murderer from the beginning, not holding to the truth, for there is no truth in him. When he lies, he speaks his native language, for he is a liar and the father of lies" (John 8:44 NIV). Remember that Jesus Christ, the Son of God, was speaking to those Jews who believed in Him and declared that they were Satan's children, not God's, and that they were living like their father, the lying murderer. Those must have seemed like harsh, shocking, even fighting words to the ears of the Jews. Israel was, after all, the only monotheistic people in the Roman world, and their claim was that they were the only ones to worship the one true God. These believers were so upset with our Lord that they would soon accuse Him, in verse 52, of being demon possessed.

Before we get there, however, let me explain what Christ was saying as best I can. Jesus is absolutely not anti-Jewish. The Jews are God's chosen people. They are dearly loved by Him. Furthermore, as the apostle Paul explained in the book of Romans, we who are Gentiles owe the Jews a great debt, for the gospel came to us through the nation of Israel. The fact is, Scripture teaches that we who were born Gentiles were also born as Satan's children. We do Satan's works and please Satan, unless, by the grace of God, we have experienced the new birth into God's family by faith in Christ, as is explained in John 3:1–18. In spite of what we may have been taught in our society, we are not born as innocent babies. God says we are born with a sin nature because we all sinned in Adam (Romans 5:12, 19). That is objective truth. Whether people believe it or not does not change the fact that God, the source of truth, said it, and that makes it true. Those who believe that objective truth is really subjective truth will, sooner or later, experience the result of faulty thinking, just as one who jumps out of a tenth-floor window will sooner or later realize he was wrong to think he could fly.

Parents do not need to teach children to do wrong, to hit, to take from other children, to lie, or to be self-centered. That comes naturally. We need to teach them to do right, to share, to be kind, and to be honest regardless of what are perceived as negative personal consequences.

I have noticed in over forty years of ministry that many of us, at one time or another, commonly believe one of Satan's lies that was first stated in the Garden of Eden. According to Genesis 3:1–6, Satan told Eve that if she wanted to be wise, she should do what he said and eat the forbidden fruit. If she did that, she would be like God. It seems to me that people, even many Christians, believe that we have three choices in life. We could be really evil, like the German dictator Adolph Hitler or like one who offers sacrifices to Satan through a satanic cult. We could be really holy, like the apostles who devoted themselves to serving God, even in the face of persecution and death. Consciously or subconsciously, we think our third choice is to be somewhere in the middle, not holier-than-thou nor a worshipper of Satan. We are, after all, independent thinkers. We decide what is best for us. We decide what is truth. We don't serve anyone. We please ourselves. We look out for number one. We often think, *It's my life, and I have a right to live it anyway I please,* or *It's my body, and I can do with it whatever I want.* We Americans often think this way because that's our culture. We are educated to do our own thing and be our own person.

One of the best expressions of this Satanic-inspired idea that humans can be independent masters of their lives is found in the poem *Invictus,* a word from the Latin meaning "unconquerable." It was composed in 1875 by the famous English humanist poet William Henley, who suffered greatly from tuberculosis. Note Henley's clear reference to the King James translation of the Bible in his fourth stanza. God says, in an obvious reference to eternal life, "Enter ye in at the strait gate: for wide *is* the gate, and broad *is* the way, that leadeth to destruction, and many there be which go in thereat: Because strait *is* the gate, and narrow *is* the way, which leadeth unto life, and few there be that find it" (Matthew 7:13–14 KJV).

Henley, like so many others in our society, including the majority of those in the halls of higher education, had a total disregard for the authority of the Word of God. Dorothea Day, a writer who lived in the early twentieth century, composed a

Christian answer to Henley's poem. Note the contrast between the two poems printed below.

Invictus	**My Captain**
By William Henley	**By: Dorothea Day**

Out of the night that covers me,	Out of the night that dazzles me,
Black as the Pit from pole to pole,	Bright as the sun from pole to pole,
I thank whatever gods may be	I thank the God I know to be
For my unconquerable soul.	For Christ the conqueror of my soul.
In the fell clutch of circumstance	Since His the sway of circumstance,
I have not winced nor cried aloud.	I would not wince nor cry aloud.
Under the bludgeonings of chance	Under that rule which men call chance
My head is bloody, but unbowed	My head with joy is humbly bowed.
Beyond this place of wrath and tears	Beyond this place of sin and tears
Looms but the Horror of the shade,	That life with Him! And His the aid,
And yet the menace of the years	Despite the menace of the years,
Finds, and shall find, me unafraid.	Keeps, and shall keep me, unafraid.
It matters not how strait the gate,	I have no fear, though strait the gate,
How charged with punishments the scroll.	He cleared from punishment the scroll.
I am the master of my fate:	Christ is the Master of my fate.
I am the captain of my soul.	Christ is the Captain of my soul

Satan successfully managed to get Eve to trust what he said rather than what the Creator said. Had Satan been honest, he would have told Eve, "When you eat of the tree, you'll belong to me." That is because, as God's Word says in Romans 6:16, we are servants of the one we choose to obey.

Dear Christian reader, let me make this as clear as I can.

We do not have three choices in life. There are only two. As created beings, humans are servants; that is our nature and our purpose in life. The question is, whom will we serve? We are commanded to serve, please, honor, worship, and love God in Deuteronomy 5, and as Moses explained to the Israelites in Deuteronomy 6:1–3, God will abundantly bless those who obey.

The apostle Paul expressed this same truth in a letter to the primarily Gentile church of Corinth: "Whether therefore ye eat, or drink, or whatsoever ye do, do all to the glory of God" (1 Corinthians 10:31 KJV). Our Lord made it clear in His famous Sermon on the Mount that humans cannot serve two masters. Prior to that sermon, He had been tempted by Satan in the wilderness of Judaea. As Matthew recorded the event, having failed in his first two attempts during the final exam, Satan took our Lord up "an exceeding high mountain." It was probably Mount Hermon, which rises over ninety-two hundred feet and is the highest peak in Palestine. There, Satan told Christ that if He would just bow down and worship him, then Satan would give Him authority over all the kingdoms of the world. In Luke 4:6 we find Satan telling Jesus that the authority over this world had been delivered to him. You remember that God had originally given that authority to Adam when he was created (Genesis 1:26). According to the principle found in Romans 6:16, he relinquished it to Satan (Luke 4:6–7) when he foolishly chose to obey him rather than the Creator.

Christ's response was superb, excellent, awesome, right on the mark. Summarizing God's commands from Deuteronomy 5:6–7, 6:13–14, 10:20, 11:13, and 13:4, Jesus told him, "Away with you,

Satan! For it is written, 'You shall worship the LORD your God, and Him only you shall serve'" (Matthew 4:10 NKJV).

Christian friend, I believe you understand Christ's reply. It's quite clear, but did it sink in to the point where you are meditating on it? God did not command us to be independent thinkers, living to please ourselves and striving for success. Satan was the first one who chose to please himself when he rebelled against his Creator. Let's be honest, especially since this book is about truth. Every time we do, say, or think anything that is contrary to our Lord's revealed will for His creation, we are rebelling exactly as Satan did when he issued his infamous "I will" declaration recorded in Isaiah 14:12–14. We are commanded, according to Philippians 2:5–11, to think like Christ and follow His example, even as Jesus lived to please the Father and was obedient to Him, regardless of the personal cost. If He hadn't been willing to submit and serve the Father, where would we be? Christ fully trusted in the words of His Father. He would gain all the kingdoms of the world, but according to Hebrews 2:14, He would acquire them God's way by defeating Satan at the cross.

Way back in Old Testament times, Joshua expressed his conviction in some of his parting words to the nation of Israel: "Now therefore, fear the LORD, serve Him in sincerity and in truth, and put away the gods which your fathers served on the other side of the River and in Egypt. Serve the LORD! And if it seems evil to you to serve the LORD, choose for yourselves this day whom you will serve, whether the gods which your fathers served that were on the other side of the River, or the gods of the Amorites, in whose land you dwell. But as for me and my house, we will serve the LORD" (Joshua 24:14–15 NKJV). We will serve just as surely as a bird is designed to fly and a fish to swim. It's our nature by creation. The question is, who is honored and pleased by how we live? Whose words will we trust? Who will we serve?

Those who are spiritually lost and blinded by Satan, as expressed in 2 Corinthians 4:3–4, will serve, please, honor, and worship the devil, even if they don't realize they are doing it. Paul pointed this out in 1 Corinthians 10:19–20, where he explained that the idol-worshipping Gentiles of his day were unknowingly offering sacrifices to the demons who were behind the idols. Centuries earlier, according to Leviticus 17:7–8 and Deuteronomy 32:15–18, Moses expressed the same truth regarding the Israelites. Forgetting their Creator, they sacrificed to pagan gods and, in doing so, unknowingly sacrificed to demons. The apostle John, when receiving the book of Revelation from Jesus Christ while exiled on the island of Patmos, recorded details of the coming tribulation period when God will pour out His wrath on the world. According to Revelation 9:13–21, following the sixth trumpet judgment, which results in the death of one-third of the world's population, those who remain alive still do not repent but rather continue to worship things that they make with their hands. As the text indicates, in doing so, they are really worshipping demons.

When our first parents, Adam and Eve, with Satan's encouragement, chose to do their own thing, they were trusting Satan rather than their Creator. Satan was served, pleased, honored, and worshipped. This is the truth that Jesus was expressing as he spoke to the religious Jews in John 8. Surely, they did not realize it. Surely, they were absolutely certain that they worshipped the one true and living God. Like some of us who were raised to be religious, attending church services regularly and perhaps even singing in the choir or teaching Sunday school, we were deceived, blinded by the great deceiver, who didn't care how religious we were as long as we weren't God's children, born into God's family through repentance of sin and faith in Christ.

Verse 45: Now getting back to John chapter 8, please look up verse 45 and carefully notice what it says, as well as what it doesn't say. This is crucial for us to understand. **Jesus did not say**, "Although I tell you the truth, you don't believe me." Perhaps we have at some time said those words to someone who questioned our honesty. Maybe it was a teacher, parent, or spouse who, because of our lack of honesty in the past, now had good reason to doubt that we were being truthful. But that is not the case here. Jesus wasn't saying "although." He said, "But **because** I tell the truth, you do not believe me" (John 8:45 ESV) (emphasis added). Now let's analyze. What kind of truth had He been telling them? Was it natural revelation; a lesson from science, math, or history, something observable in the physical world? Or was it supernatural revelation? Clearly, Jesus was speaking truth taught by God's Spirit to God's children: truth learned through faith that the unsaved human does not possess.

Verses 46–47: Jesus then asked these believing Jews two questions. He didn't wait for them to answer, for He knew they couldn't. He answered the questions Himself. And please note that the questions and answers were not primarily for their sakes but for ours. First, He asked which one of them could prove that He ever committed a sin. Obviously, they couldn't, for Jesus had lived among them as the spotless lamb of God who was therefore qualified to give His life as the sacrifice for human sin. You see, if they could have pointed to a single sin in His life, they would have had reason to doubt what He said, like the teacher who doubts the veracity of a student's statement because of past conduct.

Not being able to prove Him a sinner, they were asked a second question by Jesus: "And if I say the truth, why do ye not believe me?" (John 8:46 KJV). "And if I say the truth" in the Greek is a first-class conditional clause and can be translated, "And since I say the truth." The structure of the clause shows that the condition is real and actual, not simply possible or hypothetical. It could be translated, "If I am telling you the truth, and I am, why don't you believe Me?" His answer follows in verse 47: "Only God's children can hear His voice, and you are not His children." In other words, once again, we find that only true believers are capable of understanding supernatural revelation.

Verses 48–50: Christ's words no doubt angered them, and they reacted with a verbal attack, accusing Him of being a demon-possessed Samaritan. Christ's response was that they were dishonoring Him while He sought to honor and glorify His Father. Of course, we understand that anyone who dishonors Christ also dishonors the Father: "Whoever does not honor the Son does not honor the Father who sent Him" (John 5:23 ESV).

Verses 51–53: Jesus then made an astounding statement, again starting with a "double verily," to grab attention and signify very important truth. He proclaimed that the person who obeyed His words would never die. The Jews of course did not understand that Jesus was speaking of the true believer who, at the point of spiritual birth, according to John 5:24, "is passed from death unto life," never to be separated from God, not even by physical death (Romans 8:38–39). They replied by telling Him that if they had any doubt about His being demon-possessed, all doubt was now gone. Abraham, the greatly honored father of the Jewish nation, and the prophets of God had all experienced death. "Who do you think you are?" they replied.

Verses 54–55: The dialogue continued, with Jesus explaining that He was not honoring Himself. For humans, self-honor is worthless. Jesus is honored by His Father, the one they falsely claimed was their God, but they didn't truly know Him. Jesus continued by stating that if He denied knowing His Father, He would be lying, even as they were lying by their claim to worship God. Jesus, through submissive obedience, honored His Father while they, through their lies, honored the father of lies.

Verses 56–59: As we conclude chapter 8, we come to the vivid proof of Christ's claim that these religious Jews who were said to believe in Him in verses 30 and 31 were in reality the children of Satan, honoring the devil by acting like him and doing what pleased him. Jesus made the following statement: "Abraham rejoiced to see my day." The Greek word for "rejoiced" here means to be exceedingly glad, to jump for joy.

In all probability, this referred to the event recorded in Genesis 22, when God tested Abraham's faith and obedience by telling him to offer his beloved son Isaac, the son of promise, as a sacrifice on Mount Moriah. As Jesus many years later carried His own cross, so Isaac carried up the mountain the wood for his own sacrifice. When Isaac asked his father where the sacrificial animal was, Abraham replied, "My son, God will provide himself a lamb for a burnt offering" (Genesis 22:8 KJV). We are reminded of the words of John the Baptist, who said when he saw Jesus coming, "Behold the Lamb of God, which taketh away the sin of the world" (John 1:29 KJV).

As Abraham took the knife and was about to slay his son, the Angel of Jehovah stopped him and said, "Do not lay your hand on the lad, or do anything to him; for now I know that you fear God, since you have not withheld your son, your only son, from Me" (Genesis 22:12 NKJV). Abraham then looked up and saw that God had provided a ram caught by its horns in a thicket, and he offered it to God instead of his son.

The Angel of Jehovah spoke again to Abraham, saying, "By myself I have sworn, declares the LORD, because you have done this and have not withheld your son, your only son, I will surely bless you, and I will surely multiply your offspring as the stars of heaven and as the sand that is on the seashore. And your offspring shall possess the gate of his enemies, and in your offspring shall all the nations of the earth be blessed, because you have obeyed my voice" (Genesis 22:16–18 ESV). Put yourself in Abraham's sandals and just imagine how greatly he must have rejoiced on that eventful day, which foreshadowed the day when God would provide the Savior to take away our sin.

The Jews responded by declaring that Jesus was not even fifty, the year when people were considered to be entering old age, so how could He have seen Abraham? Jesus again used the "double verily" here to secure their attention. We could paraphrase it as, "Listen, what I'm about to tell you is extremely important and absolutely true." And then he said, "Before Abraham was, I am" (John 8:58 KJV). Note this carefully. Jesus was not simply claiming to have been alive before Abraham (though, as you know, he was). If that was all he was claiming, He would have said, "Before Abraham was, I was." No. He said, "I am," and by doing so, He identified himself as the great "I AM" who spoke to Moses in the wilderness. Remember, as recorded in Exodus 3:13–15, when Moses was commanded by God to lead the people of Israel out of the bondage they had endured in Egypt, he said to God, "When the people ask for the name of the God who sent me, what shall I tell them?"

God's reply was, "I AM WHO I AM." And He said, "Thus you shall say to the children of Israel, 'I AM has sent me to you'" (Exodus 3:14 NKJV). The Hebrew word for "I am" is the root word for Jehovah, the self-existent one, considered by Israelites to be God's holiest name. Jesus, by saying "before Abraham was, I am," was identifying Himself as Jehovah. The Jews, no doubt outraged at such a statement, then attempted to stone Him, but Jesus was hidden from them, and passing through the crowd, He left the temple. The Greek verb properly translated as "was hidden" is in the passive voice, indicating that Jesus was the recipient and not the doer of the action. Who hid Jesus from the angry mob is not stated, but we could easily assume that God the Father protected His Son, just as He did on other occasions.

As we conclude chapter 8, we find these believing Jews, whom Jesus called "liars" in verse 55 because they claimed to know and honor the one true God, showed themselves as murderers as they attempted to stone Emmanuel, God in the flesh. They were following in the steps of their father Satan, who was identified as a liar and murderer in verse 44. Jesus had proven his case.

Now I have a quick diagnostic question for you to answer in your mind. I'll tell you up front that it's a trick question, so you must think carefully about it before answering. Did the Jews understand Jesus when He said, "Before Abraham was, I am"?

Did you answer yes? If so, you probably reasoned that because they picked up stones to kill Him for His claim of equality with God, they must have understood Him. They would have considered that blasphemy and worthy of death. If your answer was no, was it because you reasoned that they would have fallen down at His feet to worship the King of kings and Lord of lords if they had really understood?

In reality, both answers are correct. Yes, they understood Him, and that is why they wanted to kill Him. However, they didn't really understand because they were unable to. They were spiritually deaf to what Jesus was teaching. They were spiritually blind to the truth. It was impossible for them to see it because of the type of truth He was declaring. He was not telling them truth that God had revealed in the natural world. In that case, they could have understood Him. Instead, He was telling them supernatural revelation, which, as we have learned from 1 Corinthians 2, is taught by God's Spirit and learned through faith, which the unsaved mind does not possess. As the apostle Paul would later declare, the Jews had a zeal for God but lacked a personal knowledge of Him.

For another vivid illustration of the fact that the unsaved mind is blind to supernatural revelation, we return to John chapter 6.

This chapter contains the feeding of the five thousand, which is the only miracle, apart from the resurrection of Christ, that is recorded in all four gospel accounts. Matthew, Mark, and Luke are commonly called "the synoptic gospels" because they give a similar synopsis (or brief overview) of Christ's life. The Gospel of John was no doubt the last gospel to be written and fills in the gaps, telling us much information not recorded by the other writers. True to form, under the inspiration of the Holy Spirit, when John recorded this miracle, he told us several things, such as the testing of Phillip, which the others omitted.

Another fact that John uniquely recorded, as found in verse 2, was the reason that the multitude was following Christ in the first place. "And a great multitude followed him, because they saw his miracles which he did on them that were diseased" (John 6:2 KJV). The three Greek verbs in this verse ("followed," "saw," and "did") are in the imperfect tense, indicating repeated action in the past. The verse could be translated as follows: "And a great multitude kept on following Him because they repeatedly saw the miracles that He continually did on those who were diseased." Jesus then took a little boy's lunch of five barley loaves and two small fish and proceeded to feed five thousand hungry men, plus the women and children who were present, until all were filled. The crowd's response to the miracle is found in verse 14: "Then those men, when they had seen the miracle that Jesus did, said, This is of a truth that prophet that should come into the world" (John 6:14 KJV).

Jesus feeding the multitude

Now, here's the question. Did the Scripture clearly say in verse 2 that the crowd followed Jesus because they saw the miracles? And according to verse 14, did they see the miracle of the loaves? Surely, the answer is yes. Why then did Jesus disagree with that conclusion, according to verse 26? "Jesus answered them, 'Truly, truly, I say to you, you are seeking me, not because you saw signs, but because you ate your fill of the loaves'" (John 6:26 ESV). Again, notice Christ's use of the double verily, which the ESV translates as "truly, truly." Once again Christ uses this phrase to cause the listeners to focus their attention on something of great significance. Note also that the apostle John used the Greek word for "sign" rather than the commonly used word *miracle,* which was employed by the synoptic writers. Jesus challenged them regarding their reason for following Him and, in doing so, instructed us on the spiritual blindness of those who are lost. The crowd was following Him not because they could read or interpret the signs, but because they liked being fed, healed, set free from demonic control, and so on. They liked what Jesus could do for them, but they would not commit themselves to Him because they did not really perceive the meaning of the signs and miracles. That will be proven to us as we proceed through chapter 6 as follows.

Verses 27–31: Using food as an illustration, Jesus told them to stop working for food that perishes and instead work for the food that would give them everlasting life. The people responded by asking Him what works God wanted them to do. Christ answered them by explaining that God required only one thing: to believe that He was the one God sent into the world. Whereupon, as is typical of the Jews, they asked Him for a sign so they could believe that He was the one, God's promised Messiah. Then, like a wife dropping an obvious hint to her husband regarding what she wants for Christmas, they suggested that He produce manna like Moses did so many years ago.

Upon reading this Scripture passage, the thoughtful person may respond to their request with the common expression, "Are you kidding me?" They had been following Jesus all over the Galilean countryside because they enjoyed seeing Him repeatedly do all sorts of miracles, and now they wanted just one more before they would believe in Him? He had just fed a crowd of more than five thousand until they were full, and now they wanted manna? Though there was no Old Testament prophecy that the Messiah would provide manna when He came, there was a common cultural belief that the Messiah would do what Moses had done.[4]

Verses 32–40: Again Jesus responded to their comments with a "double verily," as He corrected their statement regarding Moses giving manna. He pointed out that it wasn't Moses who gave their forefathers manna; it was His Father, and it was His Father who gave "the true bread from heaven." Further, Jesus explained that He himself was that bread who gave life to the world. "And Jesus said to them, 'I am the bread of life. He who comes to Me shall never hunger, and he who believes in Me shall never thirst. But I said to you that you have seen Me and yet do not believe'" (John 6:35–36 NKJV). He then explained why they did not believe in verses 37–40.

Verses 41–46: The Jews reacted to His claim that He was the bread that God sent down from heaven to give life to the world by murmuring or complaining about Him. The Greek verb is in the imperfect tense, indicating continual action. In disbelief, they repeatedly murmured to each other that they knew who His parents were, so where did He get off saying He came from heaven? Again, not that they could understand, but in verses 43–46, Jesus told them why they did not believe in Him.

Verses 47–52: Opening again with a "double verily" to emphasize great importance, Jesus made some amazing but true claims. **First**, those who believed on Him would have eternal life. **Second**, far superior to the manna their dead ancestors ate, Jesus was the living bread, and if they would eat His flesh, they would never die. **Third**, not only could Jews be saved by eating His flesh; doing so would also give eternal life to Gentiles. The reaction to His claims was predictable. The Jews continually strove, argued, and fought among themselves over what Jesus had said. Again, the verb is in the imperfect tense, indicating that a lot of arguing ensued over such astounding claims and graphic language. "How can this man give us his flesh to eat?" they said to each other (John 6:52 KJV).

Verses 53–59: According to verse 59, this address, which started in verse 26, was taking place in the synagogue at Capernaum. Jesus, for the fourth and final time in this sermon, began with the "double verily" and made the following shocking claim: "Truly, truly, I say to you, unless you eat the flesh of the Son of Man and drink his blood, you have no life in you. Whoever feeds on my flesh and drinks my blood has eternal life, and I will raise him up on the last day. For my flesh is true food, and my blood is true drink. Whoever feeds on my flesh and drinks my blood abides in me, and I in him. As the living Father sent me, and I live because of the Father, so whoever feeds on me, he also will live because of me. This is the bread that came down from heaven, not like the bread the fathers ate, and died. Whoever feeds on this bread will live forever" (John 6:53–58 ESV). (Note: For a more complete explanation of these verses, please see addendum 2.)

Verses 60–66: We can only imagine the thoughts that must have occupied their minds as they tried in vain to comprehend the meaning of His words. Christ's words seemed cannibalistic. Surely, He could not be serious. The Jews repeatedly had been commanded by God in such passages as Leviticus 17:10–14 to eat no meat that contained blood, for the life of the animal was in the blood, and God appointed it to be offered as a covering for their sin. The original commandment, however, predated the Jewish nation and went all the way back to the time of the Flood.

According to Genesis 9:1–4, when Noah and his family left the ark, they were told for the first time to eat meat but were forbidden to eat the blood of animals.

Again, the Jews' reaction to His astounding claim was predictable, and they grumbled about what He said, calling it a "hard" or "harsh saying" that was difficult for them to accept. Clearly, they could not understand it, though He clarified it for them in verse 63 when He said that He was not talking about them actually eating His literal flesh, but was speaking of devouring His words. It is trusting in the truth of His message which gives eternal life.

Jesus began His explanation in verse 61. The entire issue, for the most part, centered on the fact that they did not and could not understand who He was. He began by asking them a question: "Are you offended by what I said?" After which, He added, "Then what if you were to see the Son of Man ascending to where he was before?" (John 6:62 ESV). (Note: For an explanation of the title "Son of Man," see addendum 3.) They were thinking of Him as mere man, not as God's Son who came down from heaven. So He asked them if seeing Him return to the Father in heaven would change their thinking. The answer of course was no, and verse 65 explained why. According to Ephesians 2:8–9, we come to God by faith, and that is a gift from Him. Also the book of Hebrews teaches that "without faith it is impossible to please Him, for he who comes to God must believe that He is, and that He is a rewarder of those who diligently seek Him" (Hebrews 11:6 NKJV). Obviously, they did not have that faith. Remember that they had been following Jesus all over the place because they liked seeing the miracles. But as He said in verse 26, they didn't really see the miracles, which is proven in verse 66. The miracles showed clearly who Jesus is. Jesus is Lord of all.

Let me ask you, dear reader, if you really understood and believed that Jesus was the Creator, sustainer of life, Savior of the world, Messiah, source of all truth, and Son of the living God, would you have done what many of them did in verse 66? For that verse tells us that they left Him and never followed Him again. Why? Because they didn't truly see the miracles. The unsaved mind will superficially see supernatural revelation, but it cannot truly understand and accept it. Perhaps you have noticed how the unbelieving experts of our world are continually trying to explain away the many supernatural miracles of Scripture with naturalistic explanations. The Bible describes the unsaved as rebellious against God, deaf to spiritual truth, blinded by Satan, and dead in sin. Unless God, by His grace, gives us faith to believe and opens our eyes to see who Jesus really is, we will remain spiritually dead. As expressed in verse 65, unless God intervenes, we who were born in sin will die in our sins. "Therefore I [Jesus] said to you that you will die in your sins; for if you do not believe that I am He, you will die in your sins" (John 8:24 NKJV).

Verses 67–69: Jesus then turned to His twelve disciples and asked if they, too, were going to leave. Peter spoke up on behalf of the twelve and gave the logical answer of one whose eyes have been opened by God. (Do you remember Matthew 16:16–17?) Peter replied that Jesus was the one whose words would lead to eternal life, and they believed and were sure that He was the Messiah, God's Son.

Another passage showing the blindness of unbelievers to supernaturally revealed truth is found in Matthew 16:1–4. Jesus had, at this point, already performed countless public miracles, including most recently the feeding of the five thousand with five loaves and two fish, as recorded in chapter 14, and then the feeding of four thousand with seven loaves and a few fish, recorded in chapter 15. Now in chapter 16, some Pharisees and Sadducees confronted Him with a test. They wanted Jesus to give them some heavenly sign. His response was the same as it was back in Matthew 12:38–41 when some scribes and Pharisees asked Him for another sign.

Jesus told them, "An evil and adulterous generation seeks after a sign, and no sign will be given to it except the sign of the prophet Jonah" (Matthew 12:39 NKJV). (Note: For an explanation of His reply to them, see addendum 4.)

Though He refused to show them another sign at that time, what did He tell them? He said, "When it is evening, you say, 'It will be fair weather, for the sky is red.' And in the morning, 'It will be stormy today, for the sky is red and threatening.' You know how to interpret the appearance of the sky, but you cannot interpret the signs of the times" (Matthew 16:2–3 ESV). We have probably all heard the age-old expression "Red sky at night, sailors' delight; red sky in morning, sailors take warning." How old is that expression? No one knows, but clearly it was common knowledge at the time of Christ. Why? Because sometime in the past, sailors had learned by experience that observing weather conditions could help them predict what the weather would be like in the near future. That's natural revelation. But they were blind to the signs of the times, for that was supernatural revelation. The apostle Paul, as was mentioned earlier in 1 Corinthians chapter 2, pointed out that the leaders of that day crucified Christ because they didn't know who He was, in spite of all the signs identifying Him. The signs were all supernatural revelation.

The final evidence we will examine is found in John 10:24–27. Jesus was walking in the temple on Solomon's porch when He was approached by some Jewish leaders. They wanted Him to plainly declare that He was the Messiah, if in fact He was. It was not that they truly desired to know so that they might have followed Him. They were looking for something of which to accuse Him, as the context clearly shows, for moments later, they attempted to stone Him.

Take note of Christ's reply: "I told you, and you do not believe. The works that I do in my Father's name bear witness about me, but you do not believe because you are not among my sheep. My sheep hear my voice, and I know them, and they follow me" (John 10:25–27 ESV). They could not hear the supernatural revelation that He spoke because they were not His sheep. They were not true believers. Christ told Pilate in John 18:37 that only those who were of the truth could listen to His voice.

Once again, I remind you, as Paul explained in 1 Corinthians 2:12–14, that they could not hear because they did not have the faith by which supernatural revelation is learned. They did not possess the Spirit of God, who is the revealer and teacher of God's truth. As is recorded in John 16:13, Jesus told the disciples that the Spirit of truth would come to teach them and to reveal to them the things of the future.

CHAPTER 5

What Are the Things of God?

We now turn as promised to consider the content of **"the things of God,"** which are available to and can only be known by the true believer in Christ. (Note: For exceptions to the rule, see addendum 5.)

"But God has revealed them to us through His Spirit. For the Spirit searches all things, yes, the deep things of God. For what man knows the things of a man except the spirit of the man which is in him? Even so no one knows the things of God except the Spirit of God. Now we have received, not the spirit of the world, but the Spirit who is from God, that we might know the things that have been freely given to us by God" (1 Corinthians 2:10–12 NKJV).

First, let's be clear; we need to understand that the things of God, His ways and thoughts, are beyond man's ability to discover on his own. Job expressed in Job 9:10 that God does great things that are beyond our ability to discover. The apostle Paul later stated the same truth in his letter to the believers in Rome when he declared, "Oh, the depth of the riches both of the wisdom and knowledge of God! How unsearchable are His judgments and His ways past finding out!" (Romans 11:33 KJV). Also, God Himself speaking through the prophet Isaiah said, "'For My thoughts are not your thoughts, nor are your ways My ways,' says the LORD. 'For as the heavens are higher than the earth, so are My ways higher than your ways, and My thoughts than your thoughts'" (Isaiah 55:8–9 NKJV).

It is not possible for a created, limited human being to understand the thoughts and ways of our amazing, infinite Creator. However, our God, who can do the impossible, has chosen to gift His children with truth about His ways and plans so that, through His power, they can discern His revelations. This should be no surprise, since according to Ephesians 3:20, our God is able to do far beyond anything that man can even imagine. But often believers fail to realize what tremendous gifts we have been given. Moses expressed the fact that God reveals not all but some of His truth when he recorded in the book of Deuteronomy, "The secret things belong to the LORD our God, but the things that are revealed belong to us and to our children forever, that we may do all the words of this law" (Deuteronomy 29:29 ESV).

Our Lord Jesus, when answering the disciples' question about why He taught the multitude in parables, gave this explanation: "Because the knowledge of the secrets of the kingdom of heaven has been given to you, but not to them" (Matthew 13:11 NIV). Please notice that this knowledge of God's secrets is a gift to God's children. And as was previously stated by the apostle Paul, our God ordained, before the world was created, that we would be given this knowledge of the secret things for our glory.

However, sadly, believers are often deceived into thinking that the wisdom of this world is where truth is found, and that the Bible, God's inerrant Word, can't be fully trusted. It seems to me that that idea has been around for a long, long time. Don't you remember reading about someone encouraging Eve to be the judge of what was right and wrong because God couldn't be trusted to tell the truth? Didn't that same person suggest to Eve that God prohibited them from eating from that particular tree of knowledge because He just didn't want them to be like Him? What a liar Satan is; what a deceiver. In truth, God absolutely wants us to be like Him, but if Adam and Eve didn't trust and obey God, our Lord knew they would be rebels like Satan and would trust and obey him. Satan, whom Jesus called the father of lies in John 8:44, started with Eve and continues today to spread the same lie: that humans can be independent. "Do your own thing. Be your own person. You be the judge of what's right and wrong. You decide what's good and true for you. You're number one, if you don't look out for yourself first who will? If it feels good do it. Live for today and get all you can out of life; after all, tomorrow you may die and that's it."

The fact of the matter is, only God is independent. It is part of His divine nature to be independent and self-existent. On the other hand, all that God created, He created to glorify and serve Himself. Man, who was made in the image of God, creates things to serve himself. A piece of art, a car, a light bulb, a computer, all serve humankind and reflect glory back on the intelligent human designer.

Scripture clearly tells us that God created humankind and all that exists, in both the physical and spiritual world, to serve and glorify Himself. "The heavens declare the glory of God; and the firmament shows His handiwork" (Psalm 19:1 NKJV). "For by him were all things created, that are in heaven, and that are in earth, visible and invisible, whether they be thrones, or dominions, or principalities, or powers: all things were created by him, and for him" (Colossians 1:16 NKJV). No wonder the apostle Paul told the church of Corinth in 2 Corinthians 4:4 that Satan had blinded the minds of the unbelievers. No wonder Paul found it necessary to warn believers in the church of Colosse: "Beware lest anyone cheat you through philosophy and empty deceit, according to the tradition of men, according to the basic principles of the world, and not according to Christ" (Colossians 2:8 NKJV). Paul even found it necessary to warn Pastor Timothy, his protégé and son in the faith. "Timothy, guard what has been entrusted to your care. Turn away from godless chatter and the opposing ideas of what is falsely called knowledge, which some have professed and in so doing have departed from the faith. Grace be with you all" (1 Timothy 6:20–21 NIV).

Contrary to what Satan implied in the garden, God wants us to be like Him. How do we know that? It's part of what is given to us from the things of God. It is supernaturally revealed truth, which God's Spirit teaches believers. The fact that God wants us to be like Him is revealed to us through the Scriptures and learned through faith. For example:

1. John 13:34 tells us that we are to love one another as God loves us.

2. We are to be merciful and compassionate (Luke 6:36) like our God.

3. We are to forgive (Colossians 3:13, Ephesians 4:32) like God forgives us.

4. Those who are peacemakers (Matthew 5:9) are known as God's children.

5. We are to be perfect, mature people of integrity (Matthew 5:48), as God is perfect.

6. God is light (1 John 1:5), Jesus is the light of the world (John 8:12), and like our God, believers are called the light of the world (Matthew 5:14–16). As such, we are to shine in the midst of our crooked and corrupt generation by holding forth the life-giving words of the one true God (Philippians 2:15–16).

7. In all of our ways, we are to be holy (1 Peter 1:15–16), for our God is holy.

All that is contained in the things of God is revealed to His children in the Bible, the believer's guidebook for life. The Bible is indeed the inspired Word of the only true God. It is living, powerful, dynamic, God-revealing, self-revealing, and life-changing. It is so awesome that it is really beyond our ability to fully express in words. To be truly appreciated, it can't be just read. It has to be experienced as the genuine believer reads, meditates on, and applies its principles and commands to daily life. As our Lord Jesus expressed in John 4:31–34, our spiritual strength and daily growth comes from obeying the will of our heavenly Father. That will of God, when obeyed, brings peace beyond our understanding, regardless of the circumstances of life and fullness of joy. It is found in the holy Scriptures and is part of the things of God.

The Bible, comprised of sixty-six books, was written by approximately forty men from a wide variety of occupational backgrounds. These men, according to 2 Peter 1:16–21, were under the sovereign guidance of the Holy Spirit. On many occasions, God verbally dictated what He wanted recorded (Exodus 17:14, Jeremiah 36:2). On other occasions, God's Spirit used the language skills, style of writing, and vocabulary of the writer and guided his mind to write exactly what God wanted to communicate (1 Corinthians 14:37). While living on three different continents—Europe, Asia, and Africa—they wrote as God sovereignly directed and received revelation over a period of some fifteen hundred years. Yet the Bible, when correctly understood by the Spirit-enlightened child of God, shows a central theme woven throughout from Genesis to Revelation and evidences a beautifully designed unity. Truly, there is no other book like it; nothing comes even remotely close.

But the Bible is a large and sometimes extremely detailed book. Sometimes, it is difficult to understand. And let's be honest, there are even parts that we may think are boring. Perhaps that's because of our stage of spiritual or physical development in life, our lack of focus, our unwillingness to meditate, or simply our failure to understand the purpose of a particular portion of Scripture. But the fact remains that "all Scripture is breathed out by God and profitable for teaching, for reproof, for correction, and for training in righteousness, that the man of God may be complete, equipped for every good work" (2 Timothy 3:16–17 ESV).

Believers are often told to judge everything we are taught by the Scriptures. We are to use the Bible as a sieve and sift everything we hear and read, checking it out with what we know is the standard of truth, God's Holy Word, discarding anything that disagrees with God's truth. Isn't that precisely why the Jews in the synagogue at Berea were commended as "more noble" than those of Thessalonica? According to Acts 17:10–11, when the apostle Paul preached to them that Jesus was the Messiah, they checked his message out with the holy Scriptures to see if he was preaching the truth. No doubt his messages were similar to the ones he had preached recently for three weeks in Thessalonica. According to Acts 17:2–3, he had opened the Old Testament Scriptures and explained the Messianic prophecies to them. First, he showed them that the Messiah must experience suffering, including death. This contrasted with the Jewish mind-set, which focused only on the promises of a coming Messiah who would overthrow Rome, restore the kingdom that Israel once had, and reign forever on David's throne. Second, Paul showed them from the Scriptures, as Peter did on the day of Pentecost, that the Messiah would rise from the dead, and Jesus did exactly that. Paul's conclusion was that Jesus was indeed the promised Messiah. He probably included, as he did later in his letter to the church of Corinth (1 Corinthians

15:1–8), an accounting of all the occasions when the resurrected Christ was seen by the many eyewitnesses.

So here's a question for you: is there a shortcut? Without memorizing the Bible cover to cover, which would be a noble but very daunting task, is there an easy way to know what truth falls within the category of supernatural revelation so that the true child of God can easily and quickly recognize it? The answer clearly is yes. There is a quick computer answer or a "Cliff's Notes" version of the Bible that, in a few words, lists the content of supernatural revelation. When a believer is sitting in an atheistic professor's classroom or some unsaved expert's seminar, it is easy to discern when the experts may be speaking the truth about a subject and when they are only talking through their hat, speaking words without knowledge (i.e., speaking on a subject about which they have no true personal understanding). How does the believer know when the atheistic professor (or any unsaved person, for that matter) is speaking about a topic the unregenerate mind is spiritually unable to grasp? The answer is simple. When the unsaved speak regarding an area to which the scientific method cannot be applied, they cannot speak truth.

When they speak regarding a period of time where there is no reliable human observation and therefore no verifiable scientific testing, their hypothetical conclusions will be false. When humans choose, for whatever reason, to deny or ignore the existence and authoritative teachings of their Creator, they fulfill Romans 1:22: "Professing themselves to be wise, they became fools." As Scripture speaks of unregenerate mankind, "The fool says in his heart, 'There is no God.' They are corrupt, they do abominable deeds, there is none who does good. The LORD looks down from heaven on the children of man, to see if there are any who understand, who seek after God. They have all turned aside; together they have become corrupt; there is none who does good, not even one" (Psalm 14:1–3 ESV).

There are times when the unsaved will appear to believe some element of truth found in Scripture, but they are simply parroting supernatural revelation, which they have heard but do not personally know, comprehend, or accept. For example, the unsaved Jews in Jesus's day would absolutely proclaim that they believed in and worshipped the one true God, but they were simply parroting what they had been taught. In John 16:1–3, Jesus warned the disciples that the time would come when they would be persecuted and even murdered by those who thought they believed in and were serving God, but in reality, they didn't know God. That is exactly why the disciples would be persecuted by religious but spiritually lost Jews. That is exactly why the apostle Paul, who was highly educated in Old Testament law prior to his conversion, persecuted the early believers. That is exactly why believers down through the ages have been persecuted by those who are religious. Those who persecute know about God, but they don't personally know Him.

Now, in what could be considered the Cliff's Notes synopsis of the things of God found in supernatural revelation, the four areas that comprise such revelation are **origins, ultimate purposes, destinies**, and **morality**. In other words, humans can have no true personal knowledge of God's work, ways, and plans in these four areas unless He reveals it. And according to Scripture, He reveals these things only to His children. As has already been shown from such passages as 1 Corinthians 2:7–14, Colossians 1:16–18, and Hebrews 11:3, origins, ultimate purposes, and destinies are clearly within the sphere of supernatural revelation. (Also see the chart later in this chapter.)

Let me now address the issue of morality as the fourth aspect of supernatural revelation. While it is true according to Romans 2:14–15 that humans, via creation, have an innate knowledge of morality (our Creator's laws of right and wrong), that sense of morality was distorted by the fall of man. Sin has infected and affected every aspect of our being. Theologians refer to this as "total depravity." As a result, we humans think that we are the standard of right and wrong. Rather than submitting to the laws of our Creator who, as Creator, has the right to make the rules, we rebel and do what is right in our sight.

Satan told Eve, "Don't listen to God; trust me. Go ahead and eat the fruit, and you'll know it all. You'll know good and evil. You can be the judge." In the same way, unregenerate people today think they know what is best and refuse to submit to their Creator.

Later, God gave a written, supernatural revelation, the Ten Commandments, as recorded in Exodus 20 and Deuteronomy 5. Then He said in Deuteronomy 6, "And you shall do what is right and good in the sight of the LORD, that it may be well with you, and that you may go in and possess the good land of which the LORD swore to your fathers" (Deuteronomy 6:18 NKJV). Then Moses said to the people of Israel, "You shall not do according to all that we are doing here today, everyone doing whatever is right in his own eyes" (Deuteronomy 12:8 ESV). Moses warned

Israel again in verse 25, and then in verse 28, he said, "Be careful to obey all these words that I command you, that it may go well with you and with your children after you forever, when you do what is good and right in the sight of the LORD your God" (Deuteronomy 12:28 ESV).

The written supernatural revelation was given by God through Moses, who handed it over to Joshua. After the death of Moses, Joshua gave the following charge to the people of Israel: "This Book of the Law shall not depart from your mouth, but you shall meditate in it day and night, that you may observe to do according to all that is written in it. For then you will make your way prosperous, and then you will have good success" (Joshua 1:8 NKJV).

But for the most part, Israel did not listen. They outwardly submitted to the law of God under Joshua's leadership, but when he died, their unregenerate hearts drifted further and further from God's law. That is why it is stated twice in the book of Judges that "in those days there was no king in Israel. Everyone did what was right in his own eyes" (Judges 17:6 and 21:25 ESV). This is not simply a statement of fact; it is a statement of condemnation. God had repeatedly reminded them that His blessing on the nation was predicated upon their doing what was right in His eyes, not theirs. And remember that Israel had repeatedly promised at Mount Sinai to obey whatever God said, as long as they didn't have to get close to His awesome presence again. But they did not have ears to hear, eyes to see, or a heart to follow the one true God.

Ethics, morals, what is right, and what is wrong; where do we stand in America today? Every day, we hear someone talk about what is right. Is discrimination right? Is it right to kill an unborn baby? Is it right to call something good that the Bible calls evil? The Scripture says, "Woe unto them that call evil good, and good evil" (Isaiah 5:20 KJV). It all boils down to this all-important question: What is the standard by which something is judged right or wrong? Is the standard our conscience so that each individual is the determiner of right and wrong? Could your conscience ever be wrong? (Note: For a fuller explanation of the conscience, please see addendum 6.) Is the standard whatever the minority or the majority believe? If we can (through education, indoctrination, or brainwashing) get the majority to believe that the minority is right about something, will that make an issue that had been considered wrong now right? Is right and wrong determined by whoever shouts the loudest, by whoever is in political power, by the United Nations, by the US Supreme Court, or by the latest interpretation of the Constitution? What if everyone in the world agreed on an issue; would that settle it? The apostle Paul's answer is, "Let God be true, and every human being a liar" (Romans 3:4 NIV).

Scripture, the source of supernatural revelation, gives the following counsel: "Trust in the LORD with all your heart, And lean not on your own understanding; In all your ways acknowledge Him, And He shall direct your paths. Do not be wise in your own eyes; Fear the LORD and depart from evil" (Proverbs 3:5–7 NKJV). "The way of a fool is right in his own eyes, But he who heeds counsel is wise" (Proverbs 12:15 NKJV). "Every way of a man is right in his own eyes, But the LORD weighs the hearts" (Proverbs 21:2 NKJV). "He who trusts in his own heart is a fool, But whoever walks wisely will be delivered" (Proverbs 28:26 NKJV).

These truths regarding origins, ultimate purposes, destinies, and God's moral standards for His creation are impossible for humans to discover on their own in the natural world. Job expressed this fact in the following passage: "He alone spreads out the heavens, And treads on the waves of the sea; He made the Bear, Orion, and the Pleiades, And the chambers of the south; He does great things past finding out, Yes, wonders without number" (Job 9:8–10 NKJV).

The apostle Paul echoes the same fact in his letter to the believers in Rome: "Oh, the depth of the riches both of the wisdom and knowledge of God! How unsearchable *are* His judgments and His ways past finding out!" (Romans 11:33 NKJV).

Supernatural revelation may be defined as "that act of God by which He communicates to the mind of man truth not known before and incapable of being discovered by the mind of man unaided."[5] The following chart may help to visualize the biblical philosophy of truth which has been presented in this book.

Two kinds of objective truth:	Natural revelation	Supernatural revelation
Found in:	Nature	God's Word
Learned through:	The five senses with human reasoning via experience and research	**Faith**, and the teacher is **God's Spirit**
Content of:	God's truth discovered in the natural world	1. **Origins** 2. **Purposes** 3. **Destinies** 4. **Morals**
Available to:	Everyone	**Believers only**

CHAPTER 6

So What? How Does This Affect the Believer's Life?

For the true believer, born again by the grace of God, what are the ramifications, applications, consequences, and results of clearly understanding these great truths? For those who hold fast to their faith and trust in the words of the one true God, He provides peace, mental and spiritual protection for the present, direction, comfort, and a sure and certain hope of an everlasting future as a joint-heir with Christ.

Understanding the biblical philosophy of supernatural revelation results in at least three important benefits for God's children:

First, it causes us to appreciate one of the many great blessings that our heavenly Father gives to His children. We have God's truth, and by God's grace, only we can really understand it.

"And those who know Your name will put their trust in You;

For You, LORD, have not forsaken those who seek You" (Psalm 9:10 NKJV).

"I have manifested Your name to the men whom You have given Me out of the world. They were Yours, You gave them to Me, and they have kept Your word" (John 17:6 NKJV).

"For I have given them the words that you gave me, and they have received them and have come to know in truth that I came from you; and they have believed that you sent me" (John 17:8 NKJV).

"It is given unto you to know the mysteries of the kingdom of heaven, but to them [the unsaved] it is not given" (Matthew 13:11 KJV).

"But we speak the wisdom of God in a mystery, the hidden wisdom which God ordained before the ages for our glory" (1 Corinthians 2:7 NKJV).

Second, it helps us to realize why the unsaved world cannot perceive the truth that seems so obvious to us.

"Why do you not understand My speech? Because you are not able to listen to My word" (John 8:43 NKJV).

"But because I tell the truth [supernatural revelation], you do not believe Me" (John 8:45 NKJV).

"He who is of God hears God's words; therefore you do not hear, because you are not of God" (John 8:47 NKJV).

"Jesus answered them, 'I told you, and you do not believe. The works that I do in My Father's name, they bear witness of Me. But you do not believe, because you are not of My sheep, as I said to you. My sheep hear My voice, and I know them, and they follow Me'" (John 10: 25–27 NKJV).

Third, it protects us against the very real danger of being led astray into the many false philosophies of our American culture.

What false views of life are common in our culture today and are totally contrary to the truths of Scripture? Let me list a few:

A. You are number one.

B. You're worth it; you deserve it.

C. You have your rights, and no one has the right to tell you how to live.

D. Follow your heart, and you won't go wrong.

E. If it feels right, do it.

F. If you can dream it, you can do it. Follow your dreams.

G. Atheistic evolution is the true explanation of nature's existence.

Remember that the apostle Paul gave two clear warnings about the danger of listening to the world's wisdom rather than God's wisdom: "See to it that no one takes you captive through hollow and deceptive philosophy, which depends on human tradition and the basic principles of this world rather than on Christ" (Colossians 2:8 NIV). "Timothy, guard what has been entrusted to your care. Turn away from godless chatter and the opposing ideas of what is falsely called knowledge, which some have professed and in so doing have wandered from the faith. Grace be with you" (1 Timothy 6:20–21 NIV).

The apostle Peter also gave clear warning in the following two passages. "But there were also false prophets among the people, just as there will be false teachers among you. They will secretly introduce destructive heresies, even denying the sovereign Lord who bought them—bringing swift destruction on themselves. Many will follow their depraved conduct and will bring the way of truth into disrepute. In their greed these teachers will exploit you with fabricated stories. Their condemnation has long been hanging over them, and their destruction has not been sleeping." (1 Peter 2:1-3 NIV). Therefore, dear friends, since you have been forewarned, be on your guard so that you may not be carried away by the error of the lawless and fall from your secure position. But grow in the grace and knowledge of our Lord and Savior Jesus Christ. To him be glory both now and forever! Amen. (2 Peter 3:17-18 NIV).

Christian friend, if you are being tempted by the words and ways of the world, please listen to the words of God spoken through Jeremiah the prophet. God said in Jeremiah 5:5 that the backsliding Jews were foolish because they were not following God's way. In Jeremiah 6:10, He said that His Word was an object of scorn to them rather than an object in which they found delight. Again He warned the Jews, saying, "Behold, ye trust in lying words, that cannot profit" (Jeremiah 7:8 KJV). In Jeremiah 8:9, the Lord said the Jews had no wisdom because they rejected His Word. In a solemn warning, our Creator said, "Hear, O earth: behold, I will bring evil upon this people, *even* the fruit of their thoughts, because they have not hearkened unto my words, nor to my law, but rejected it" (Jeremiah 6:19 KJV).

Believers, don't be swayed by the spiritually blind professor;

the pseudo-intellectual; the eloquent, charismatic speaker; or the scientist who is wise in his own eyes but doesn't even truly know where he came from or where he is going because he doesn't know the Creator. Do not be swayed by the teachings of those who speak words without knowledge. Be wary of those who, as the apostle Paul says, are "always learning and never able to come to the knowledge of the truth" (2 Timothy 3:7 NKJV). If, according to Matthew 4:4, the perfect, holy Son of God told Satan that man shall live by trusting in every word that God speaks, is it ever a good idea to follow Adam and Eve's example and believe that God is lying and someone else is telling us the truth? In Matthew 23:13 and Luke 11:52, our Lord denounces teachers who are not entering God's kingdom themselves and are a hindrance to those who want to enter. Specifically, Christ says in Luke that these teachers "have taken away the Key of knowledge," which, as has been shown, is the fear of the LORD.

The apostle John, who was the last of the apostles to leave this earth, wrote the following passage to warn his fellow believers regarding who they should and shouldn't believe. The words of the Holy Spirit through John form an appropriate ending to this book. In them, God warned us not to listen to or accept the teachings of those who do not have a personal relationship with God the Father through faith in Jesus Christ. I refer, of course, to the occasions when those who are of the world are teaching on the things contained in special revelation, for Scripture declares that the things of God are revealed only to His children. When the unsaved are teaching what has been discovered in our world through natural revelation, we should listen, learn about, and appreciate what our great God has created. When the unsaved are speaking words without knowledge from the area of origins, ultimate purposes, destinies, and morality, we need to be careful to trust the words of the God who created us, for He alone is the judge of all the world. If our eyes are open to His truth, and we are thinking biblically, we will not be led astray by one who possesses the spirit of error.

God's Word gives ample and stern warning to believers about listening to those who do not know the supernaturally revealed truth taught by the Spirit. So why listen to liars who lead you astray and lull you to sleep as they attempt to undermine your faith? The apostle John put it this way: "I have not written to you because you do not know the truth, but because you know it, and that no lie is of the truth. Who is a liar but he who denies that Jesus is the Christ? He is antichrist who denies the Father and the Son. Whoever denies the Son does not have the Father either; he who acknowledges the Son has the Father also. Therefore let that abide in you which you heard from the beginning. If what you heard from the beginning abides in you, you also will abide in the Son and in the Father. And this is the promise that He has promised us—eternal life. These things I have written to you concerning those who try to deceive you" (1 John 2:21–26 NKJV). "Beloved, do not believe every spirit, but test the spirits, whether they are of God; because many false prophets have gone out into the world. By this you know the Spirit of God: Every spirit that confesses that Jesus Christ has come in the flesh is of God, and every spirit that does not confess that Jesus Christ has come in the flesh is not of God. And this is the spirit of the Antichrist, which you have heard was coming, and is now already in the world. You are of God, little children, and have overcome them, because He who is in you is greater than he who is in the world. They are of the world. Therefore they speak as of the world, and the world hears them. We are of God. He who knows God hears us; he who is not of God does not hear us. By this we know the spirit of truth and the spirit of error" (1 John 4:1–6 NKJV).

What Does It Mean to Fear the Lord?

To fear the Lord is first and foremost to be afraid of disobeying Him because of the consequences. Scriptures contain several examples, such as the one found in Joshua 22, where the Jewish tribal leaders reminded their brothers of God's recent judgment for rebellion, in which twenty-four thousand Israelites were killed. Obedience initially may be borne out of fear. Later, with maturity, it may come out of a heart of love. The Israelites needed to learn to trust God, to honor, to respect, and to love Him with their whole hearts. Proverbs 3:5–7 reveals that the fear of the Lord includes trusting in what He says rather than in what we may think. According to Job 28:12–28 and Proverbs 8:13, it also means that we will love what God loves and hate what He hates.

What is the fear of the Lord? A study of the following passages should help us:

1. It is required by God; it's not just a suggestion (Deuteronomy 10:12–13).

2. It is something that must be taught (Psalm 34:11).
3. It is learned by a study of the Scriptures (Deuteronomy 17:14–20).
4. It is a choice that we make (Proverbs 1:20, 24–33).
5. God promises us understanding of it if we will obey Him and diligently seek His wisdom and knowledge (Proverbs 2:1–6).

There are great benefits for those who fear the Lord. Solomon summarized it this way: "By humility and the fear of the LORD are riches, and honor, and life" (Proverbs 22:4 KJV). Some of those blessings are listed below:

1. The fear of the Lord protects us from the consequences of sin (Proverbs 14:27, 16:6).
2. God gives His personal attention to those who fear Him (Psalm 33:18–19).
3. God promises us His protection so that if we fear the Lord, we don't need to fear anything else in life (Psalm 33:18–20, 34:6–7, 56:4; Proverbs 14:26, 29:25).
4. He promises to provide for all our needs (Psalm 34:9–10).
5. He grants us a prolonged life (Proverbs 9:10–11, 10:27, 14:27; Deuteronomy 6:1–2).
6. The Lord gives peace to those who fear Him (Proverbs 1:29–33, 16:7).
7. He even gives posthumous blessings for our family (Proverbs 11:21; 2 Kings 4:1–7).

The wisdom of Solomon directed us in some of his first recorded teachings: "The fear of the LORD is the beginning of knowledge; fools despise wisdom and instruction" (Proverbs 1:7 ESV). In Solomon's final words of wisdom, he said, "The end of the matter; all has been heard. Fear God and keep his commandments, for this is the whole duty of man" (Ecclesiastes 12:13 ESV). It sounds to me like no one can be truly successful in life, as God counts success, and possess true wisdom and knowledge without the fear of the Lord.

What Did Jesus Mean When He Told the Jews that They Must Eat His Flesh and Drink His Blood in Order to Have Eternal Life, According to John 6:53, 54?

This is also one of the commonly misunderstood passages of Scripture. As previously stated, the synoptic gospels of Matthew, Mark, and Luke give a similar overview or synopsis of Christ's life. Each of them recorded the institution of the Lord's Supper during that Passover meal called the Last Supper. Jesus and His disciples celebrated it in Jerusalem in the upper room the night prior to His crucifixion. John's gospel gave the account of the Last Supper in chapter 13. John, however, made no mention of the Lord's Supper that believers are to continually observe, remembering His death until He returns.

Some believe that the ordinance of the Lord's Supper was too important for John to have omitted it from his gospel account. They suggest that this was what Christ was speaking about in the bread of life discourse recorded in John chapter 6. In other words, when Jesus told the Jews that they needed to eat His flesh and drink His blood, He was primarily referring to what we call the communion service. That view, however, is absolutely incorrect. The evidence from the text clearly shows that John was recording another illustration to support his purpose in writing, which was stated in John 20:30–31. There, he explained that he was writing to prove that Jesus was the Messiah, God's Son, so that people may trust in Him and be saved from their sin.

John recorded illustration after illustration of what it meant to truly believe, to have real faith in Christ. In chapter 3, John showed Jesus using the illustration of being born again as He was talking to Nicodemus. In chapter 4, Jesus talked to the Samaritan woman at Jacob's well. Jesus didn't tell her that she needed to be born again. He told her that she should ask Him for the gift of living water, and she would never be thirsty again. In chapter 6, a different illustration was used, probably the most vivid illustration recorded in Scripture to explain what it means to trust in Christ. As Jesus delivered His synagogue message, He told the Jews that in order to have eternal life, they had to eat His flesh and drink His blood. King David expressed a similar salvation illustration in the Old Testament when he said, "Oh, taste and see that the LORD *is* good; Blessed *is* the man *who* trusts in Him!" (Psalm 34:8 NKJV).

In John 6:53, the verbs "eat" and "drink" are in the Greek aorist tense, indicating completed action at a point in time, not repeated action, as would be required if the ordinance of communion was what Jesus had in mind. Another difference between this illustration and the communion service (the Lord's Supper) is that Jesus used the word "flesh" on this occasion, but the synoptic gospels record him using the word "body" when introducing the Lord's Supper. Of course, the strongest argument against the belief that Jesus was referring to the communion service is the fact that the partaking of communion does not save us, for we are saved by God's grace through faith alone, and not by any human act, such as taking communion.

Two final comments are relevant here. First, according to Romans 6:3–5, the Lord's Supper uses similar terminology to the communion service because it is a picture of the salvation experience, just as the water baptism of a new believer is a picture of the baptism of the Spirit joining us with Christ in his death, burial, and resurrection. Second, when considering the idea that the Lord's Supper is too important to be left out of John's gospel, we need to remember that, to a large extent, John was filling in information about Christ that the synoptics omitted. Much of the Christology in John's gospel is unique to John. For instance, the second miraculous catch of fish and the restoration of Peter after Christ's resurrection are only recorded by John. The longest recorded prayer of Christ is found only in John 17. Also, of the seven miraculous signs recorded by John, five are unique to his account. It would not at all be unusual for John to leave out the institution of the Lord's Supper, since it had already been recorded three times.

Why Did Jesus Commonly Refer to Himself as the "Son of Man," and What Is the Meaning of the Title?

I am indebted to the late Dr. Leon Morris, a great Bible scholar and author of *The Gospel According to John* volume of *The New International Commentary on the New Testament* (edited by F. F. Bruce, 1971) for helping me to comprehend its meaning.

The expression "son of Man" is first found in Numbers 23:19, where God declared that He was not the son of Man. Since God does not have a human nature, He does not lie or change His mind, as we humans do. The expression is commonly used in the Old Testament as a synonym for "human being" and is used by God when referring to such men as Daniel and Ezekiel. The same phrase, "Son of Man," became a frequently used title by our Lord when He came to earth and is another often misunderstood expression. The phrase is found eighty-two times in the gospels, for Jesus constantly referred to Himself as the Son of Man.

The apostle Peter, having received revelation from God the Father, answered our Lord's question correctly. "When Jesus came into the region of Caesarea Philippi, He asked His disciples, saying, 'Who do men say that I, the Son of Man, am?' So they said, 'Some say John the Baptist, some Elijah, and others Jeremiah or one of the prophets.' He said to them, 'But who do you say that I am?' Simon Peter answered and said, 'You are the Christ [the Messiah], the Son of the living God.' Jesus answered and said to him, 'Blessed are you, Simon Bar-Jonah, for flesh and blood has not revealed *this* to you, but My Father who is in heaven'" (Matthew 16:13–17 NKJV). It is worth noting that the word "Christ" comes from the Greek, and "Messiah" comes from the Hebrew language. The words are synonyms and mean "the anointed" or "appointed one." Jesus is God's anointed/appointed one, sent by Him to deliver us from sin.

Others never call Jesus the Son of Man, nor do they use the expression, except on one occasion in John 12:34. There, following the triumphal entrance into Jerusalem on Palm Sunday, Jesus was asked by the people to explain what He meant when He called Himself the Son of Man. That one verse gives insight as to why Jesus so often referred to Himself that way. It was precisely because people didn't understand His usage of it that He chose it. For one thing, it was not a politically charged term. It was non-offensive and seemingly just a generic term for a human being. That is exactly what it meant in the vast majority of its Old Testament occurrences. But when Jesus came to this earth and called Himself the Son of Man, He was really proclaiming that He was God's Messiah.

As we read Scripture, we often gloss over the phrase and assume that Jesus was simply identifying Himself as one who partook of the human nature, a human being. However, when we study the New Testament contexts in which Jesus calls Himself the Son of Man, it becomes clear that, though He was fully human as well as fully God, He was not using the expression primarily to claim humanity for Himself. Rather, He was using the phrase as a Messianic title. Clearly, Jesus would not have had the freedom to travel around the country teaching and preaching as He did if He publicly announced to the crowds that He was the Messiah sent by God. The Roman and Jewish establishments would have been seeking to kill Him from day one, just as Herod the Great did upon hearing of His birth. Instead, He let His works prove that He was the Messiah for those who had eyes to see and ears to hear. An example of this can be found in John 10:22–27. How different this scenario is from the individuals running around our world today who with their words claim to be the Messiah, but their lives and works prove otherwise.

Looking at the New Testament contexts in which the title is used reveals to us the Messianic connection to the title. Because Jesus is the Son of Man, the following Messianic truths are associated with Him:

1. He preexisted with God the Father prior to coming to earth (John 3:13, 6:62).
2. He is God's Son, and as such, He has the power to forgive sin and save us (Luke 5:24, 9:56, 19:10; John 3:14–16, 6:53).

3. He has the right and power to judge humankind (Matthew 16:27; John 5:27).

4. He is seated at God's right hand and will come in His kingdom (Matthew 16:28; Luke 22:69).

If the phrase "Son of Man" meant nothing more than that Jesus was human, then we who are also humans preexisted with the Father before we came to earth. We, too, can forgive sin, save others, and judge the world simply because we are human. But this, of course, is not the case. It appears that Jesus took a common phrase out of the Old Testament, perhaps from a Messianic prophecy such as Psalm 80:17. Perhaps He took it from Daniel 7:13, where Daniel sees a vision of "one who looked like the son of man," a human, receiving a kingdom from the Ancient of days (God the Father), and used it as a Messianic title referring to Himself. If, as we read through the gospels, we replace the phrase "Son of Man" with the word "Messiah," we find that it fits perfectly.

Why Wouldn't Jesus Grant the Leaders' Request to See a sign? What is the meaning of the one sign He gave the leadership?

The educated religious leadership of the nation, the priests, scribes, Pharisees, and Sadducees, above all people, should have known that the giving of miraculous signs was one of the primary tests of a prophet of God. That's why the Jews as a nation were always looking for signs (1 Corinthians 1:22; Deuteronomy 18:15–22). All the way back from the time of Moses, God authenticated His spokesmen by giving them miraculous powers to produce signs and wonders, so that Israel would listen and obey. The true prophets spoke for God, and according to such passages as Exodus 19:7–8, 20:18–19, 24:3, and 24:7, Israel repeatedly promised to obey whatever God said, whether He spoke through Moses or one of his successors. The nation of Israel was absolutely terrified when God came down and spoke with a great display of power from Mount Sinai. In their fear of God, they asked Moses to be their go-between, promising to obey whatever God told him. They were afraid that they would all die if they got that close to God again.

Approximately fourteen hundred years later, according to Hebrews 1:1–2 and 2:3–4, God spoke through His Son and through eyewitnesses of His life, death, and resurrection. Again, God authenticated their message through miraculous signs. Jesus, in fact, did so many miracles that, as it is recorded in John 7:31, some of the Jews who truly believed said He must be the Messiah, since it was unthinkable that someone else could do more miracles than Jesus had done. Why then wouldn't Jesus let these religious leaders see one more sign, and why did He call them "an evil and adulterous generation"? The answer is that Jewish leadership was guilty of spiritual adultery. They claimed to be faithful to Jehovah God, but in reality, they refused to submit to Him. The Sanhedrin, Israel's ruling body of religious leadership, in a self-condemning statement, even admitted in John 11:47 that Jesus had done many miracles, but they refused to obey His message from God the Father. According to John 11:47–50, it was in fact on this occasion that Caiaphas, the high priest, hatched the plan to execute Christ. Sadly, "although He had done so many signs before them, they did not believe in Him" (John 12:37 NKJV). What was the message that God was sending to Israel at this crucial time in history? What did Jehovah want them to do? The answer is clearly stated in John 6:28–29 when the Jews asked Jesus what God wanted of them. Jesus replied by saying that God only required one thing. He wanted them to believe that He was the Messiah sent from God.

As to the sign He gave them, it was the sign of the prophet Jonah. As Jonah was in the belly of the fish for three days and nights, so Christ would be in the grave for three days and nights. Then, just like Jonah, He would be back. It was the same sign that He gave them when they were so upset after His first cleansing of the temple. It was at the beginning of His ministry, as recorded in John 2:14–21, and the Jewish leadership asked him for a sign. In other words, they were asking what right He had to cleanse the temple because a sign would indicate that He was a prophet of God. It is interesting to me that they didn't say He was wrong for driving out the animals and money changers. They only asked for the proof of His authority. His response was, "Destroy this temple, and in three days I will raise it up" (John 2:19 KJV).

Of course, they assumed He was talking about the immensely impressive stone temple that, by Herod's order, had been in the process of being remodeled for the past forty-six years. To rebuild it in only three days must have seemed to them both absurd and impossible. But, as John points out in verse 21, Jesus was speaking of the crucifixion and resurrection of His body, for He was Emmanuel, God's temple in the flesh. Far greater than rebuilding Herod's temple in three days, far greater than they could ever begin to imagine, Christ's resurrection conquered sin, Satan, and death and secured God's plan of redemption for the human race. They asked for proof of his authority. They didn't and couldn't understand it, for He was speaking supernatural revelation. Jesus gave them the sign of the resurrection which, according to Romans 1:4, proved He was God's Son. What right did he have to clean out God's place of worship in Jerusalem? Far greater than the right of one who was only a human prophet; Jesus is God's Son, and the temple was His Father's house.

Is the Natural or Unsaved Man Ever Permitted by God to Understand Supernatural Revelation?

The natural or unsaved man that Paul described in 1 Corinthians 2:14 clearly was not able to truly understand supernatural revelation, or what the Scriptures referred to as "the things of God." As has been shown, such truths are learned through faith and taught by God's Spirit. But there is an exception to the rule, and that is when God by His grace is drawing the unsaved to Himself, granting them faith by which to understand God's Word, repent of sin, and receive the gift of eternal life. This is often, and perhaps always, a process by which God increases an individual's knowledge and understanding of who Jesus is over time, until the point of salvation is reached. Illustrations of this can be found in the life of the Samaritan woman at the well, recorded in the Gospel of John chapter 4, and in the healing and conversion of the man who was born blind in John chapter 9. There are two things to keep in mind. First, as God declared in Isaiah 55:11, when He sends His Word out, it always accomplishes His purpose. Second, one of God's purposes is to give faith to individuals who are spiritually dead. In Romans 10:13–17, Paul explained that the process by which God gives faith to us is through the hearing of His all-powerful, life-changing Word.

Another example of an exception may be found in the God-given revelation to the great Babylonian king, Nebuchadnezzar, as recorded in Daniel chapter 2. There, the pagan king was given a dream by God, and Daniel was empowered by God to interpret it for him so that the king might know the meaning of what he had dreamed. In that dream, God revealed His plans for future kingdoms to rise in power and subdue the previous world powers, until God would establish Christ's eternal reign of righteousness on the earth. Nebuchadnezzar dreamed of a statue comprised of different metals, described from head to toe in descending order of value but ascending degrees of strength. It was revealed to the king that he and his kingdom were represented by the head of gold. The feet of the image were struck by a stone, resulting in the obliteration of the entire image. The stone then became a mountain that filled the whole earth. God gave additional revelations to Nebuchadnezzar in chapters 2 and 3.

Whether or not these revelations were for the purpose of the king's salvation is debatable, since there are indications in chapter 4 that he became a believer in the one true God, but there is also evidence that he did not. The primary purpose of the revelations, however, is clear from the book of Daniel. They are recorded so that true believers might know that regardless of how things might look here on earth, all of history will work out according to the sovereign rule of God, who has planned the end from the beginning and is in full and absolute control. As God declares, "Remember the former things of old, For I am God, and there is no other; I am God, and there is none like Me, Declaring the end from the beginning, And from ancient times things that are not yet done, Saying, 'My counsel shall stand, And I will do all My pleasure'" (Isaiah 46:9–10 NKJV).

ADDENDUM 6

What Is a Conscience?

Is a conscience the voice of the Holy Spirit telling us what is right and wrong? Is our conscience infallible? Is it always trustworthy and incapable of making an error in judgment? Can our conscience change so that the inner voice that said what was right or wrong in the past now says the opposite? Is it the voice of Jiminy Cricket from Walt Disney's famous film *Pinocchio?* Viewers were instructed in the film and children have often been told to let their conscience be their guide. But is it true that if we follow our conscience, we will never go wrong?

The only place where we could find the correct answers to these questions would be in the Instruction Manual written by the God who created us. Scripture clearly reveals that our conscience is not the Holy Spirit speaking to us; the unsaved do not possess God's Spirit, but they do have a conscience that can convict them of sin (John 8:9). The Spirit may use a person's conscience (Romans 9:1; John 16:7–11), but He is not the conscience. Scripture also tells us that a conscience can be weak (1 Corinthians 8:12), defiled (Titus 1:15), evil (Hebrews 10:22), and seared, making it hardened or insensitive (1 Timothy 4:2). Conversely, Scripture tells us that a conscience can be described as good (Acts 23:1), void of offense (Acts 24:16), pure (2 Timothy 1:3), and perfect (Hebrews 9:9). A conscience can also be changed (Hebrews 9:14, 10:22). By way of illustration, consider how the conscience of individuals in our country, as shown by national studies, polls, and ballot results, has changed during the last two hundred years on such topics as slavery, abortion, adultery, divorce, marriage, premarital sex, voting rights, homosexuality, and recreational drug use.

To define the word *conscience*, we need only to go to the Greek word in the New Testament, which is transliterated "*syneidesis.*" Looking at its etymology, it is a compound word that essentially means "with knowledge." Romans 2:15 and 9:1 demonstrate that a conscience speaks to a person, for it "bears witness." The conscience has often been described as our moral compass. It could be defined as the voice of our moral standard, which commends or condemns our thoughts and actions. It bears witness according to the knowledge of right and wrong that we have been taught as children. That is why it is so vitally important to teach children God's moral standard at an early age so that it becomes an integral part of their conscience. And why is that important? Christian parents naturally want their children to trust in Christ and be saved from the consequences of sin at an early age. While the moral law of God cannot save anyone, for according to Romans 3:20 that was never its purpose, it does show us that we are all sinners in need of salvation. Realizing this fact is the first step toward repentance, so that the child can call out to Christ for the gift of salvation.

A few final but very important notes regarding the conscience:

1. Our conscience can change or develop over time with the addition of moral knowledge (i.e., knowledge regarding what is right or wrong). If that knowledge is not according to God's truth, for He is the source and standard of truth, then our conscience will be adversely affected.

2. A clear conscience is possible only through the sacrifice of Christ, who paid the penalty for our sin (Hebrews 10:1–14).

3. In order for a believer to properly honor and serve God, it is necessary to have a clear or clean conscience (Hebrews 9:14; 2 Timothy 1:3; Psalm 66:18; Proverbs 28:13; Isaiah 59:1–2).

4. The apostles Paul and Peter both told us that a clear conscience is a spiritual weapon (1 Timothy 1:18–20; 1 Peter 3:15–16; 2 Corinthians 10:3–5).

5. A clear conscience is obtained through reconciliation (2 Chronicles 7:12–14). Reconciliation may be defined as healing a broken relationship by settling a dispute. Believers who have broken fellowship with the Lord due to disobedience can be restored through the simple act of repentance and confession, as expressed in the following passage: "If we confess our sins, he is faithful and just to forgive us our sins, and to cleanse us from all unrighteousness" (1 John 1:9 KJV). This verse has often been quoted as one that shows how an individual might be saved, but the context clearly indicates that it is written to

believers to show them how to be restored to fellowship with God. God is faithful to keep the promises of forgiveness contained in His Word. He is just in forgiving us because Jesus has already paid the penalty for our sin, and we who have become God's children through faith in Christ need only to confess and turn from our sin to be restored to fellowship. Jesus expressed this same truth in John 13:10, when He told Peter that one who has already taken a bath needs to wash only his feet (i.e., one who is already saved only needs to confess daily sin to restore fellowship with God). In the same sense, a child who disobeys a parent only needs to confess and obey to have fellowship restored. The child does not need to be born into the family again.

6. The apostle Paul expressed the importance of serving the Lord with a clear conscience when he said, "So I strive always to keep my conscience clear before God and man" (Acts 24:16 NIV). Paul worked at maintaining a clear conscience. We must do the same if we want to enjoy all of the benefits of being in fellowship with our heavenly Father, and if we want to bring honor to the LORD Jesus to whom we owe absolutely everything.

EPILOGUE

Dear reader, this book was written primarily for the benefit of true Christians, those who have repented of sin and accepted God's gift of salvation and forgiveness by trusting in Christ as their Lord and Savior. If, by God's sovereign plan, you read all the way to the end of this book and realized that you do not have a personal relationship with the God who created you, then please carefully consider the following truths from Scripture:

The one who created us and all that exists is absolutely holy. "And one [angel] cried unto another, and said, Holy, holy, holy, is the LORD of hosts: the whole earth is full of his glory" (Isaiah 6:3 KJV). King David said, "Bless the LORD, O my soul: and all that is within me, bless his holy name" (Psalm 103:1 KJV).

All of humanity has sinned against our holy God, and as such, we are deserving of eternal punishment. "As it is written, There is none righteous, no, not one" (Romans 3:10 KJV). "For all have sinned, and come short of the glory of God" (Romans 3:23 KJV). "The soul that sinneth, it shall die" (Ezekiel 18:20 KJV). "And whosoever was not found written in the book of life was cast into the lake of fire" (Revelation 20:15 KJV).

God is also a God of love and grace. He therefore provided

a way for us to escape the just punishment for sin that we deserve. "For by grace are ye saved through faith; and that not of yourselves: it is the gift of God: not of works, lest any man should boast" (Ephesians 2:8–9 KJV). "This is love: not that we loved God, but that he loved us and sent his Son as an atoning sacrifice for our sins" (1 John 4:10 NIV). "But God demonstrates His own love toward us, in that while we were still sinners, Christ died for us" (Romans 5:8 NKJV).

God sent His Son, the Lord Jesus Christ, into the world to provide a solution to our sin problem. He lived a perfect life and then took both our sin and the punishment we deserved upon Himself, dying in our place on a Roman cross.

"For we do not have a High Priest who cannot sympathize with our weaknesses, but was in all points tempted as we are, yet without sin" (Hebrews 4:15 NKJV). "Do not think that I came to destroy the Law or the Prophets. I did not come to destroy but to fulfill" (Matthew 5:17 NKJV).

"For God sent not his Son into the world to condemn the world; but that the world through him might be saved" (John 3:17 KJV). "Who his own self bare our sins in his own body on the tree, that we, being dead to sins, should live unto righteousness: by whose stripes ye were healed" (1 Peter 2:24 KJV). "For He hath made him to be sin for us, who knew no sin; that we might be made the righteousness of God in him" (2 Corinthians 5:21 KJV).

Trusting in Christ is God's one and only plan for salvation and our only hope. If you do not believe in the words of God, you must bear the consequences of your sin. Probably the most famous verse in the Bible is John 3:16, which tells us that if we put our faith in Christ, we won't perish. But the converse is that if we don't believe, we will perish. "He who believes in Him is not condemned; but he who does not believe is condemned already, because he has not believed in the name of the only begotten Son of God" (John 3:18 NKJV). Jesus said, "I am the way, the truth, and the life. No one comes to the Father except through Me" (John 14:6 NKJV). "Enter through the narrow gate. For wide is the gate and broad is the road that leads to destruction, and many enter through it. But small is the gate and narrow the road that leads to life, and only a few find it" (Matthew 7:13–14 NIV). "He who believes in the Son has everlasting life; and he who does not believe the Son shall not see life, but the wrath of God abides on him" (John 3:36 NKJV). "Truly, these times of ignorance God overlooked, but now commands all men everywhere to repent, because He has appointed a day on which He will judge the world in righteousness by the Man whom He has ordained. He has given assurance of this to all by raising Him from the dead" (Acts 17:30–31 NKJV).

The word *gospel* means "good news," and God's good news is that He loves you and wants to give the free gift of salvation to all who will accept it. All you need to do is repent of your sin and ask Christ to save you. The apostle Paul preached "both to the Jews, and also to the Greeks, repentance toward God, and faith toward our Lord Jesus Christ" (Acts 20:21 KJV). "For the wages of sin is death; but the gift of God is eternal life through Jesus Christ our Lord" (Romans 6:23 KJV). "For whosoever shall call upon the name of the Lord shall be saved" (Romans 10:13 KJV). "If you confess with your mouth the Lord Jesus and believe in your heart that God has raised Him from the dead, you will be saved. For with the heart one believes unto righteousness, and with the mouth confession is made unto salvation" (Romans 10:9–10 NKJV).

If you, from the heart, have responded to God's command to repent of sin and have prayed, asking Christ to forgive and save you and to become the Lord of your life, then you are now a child of God by faith in His Son. 2 Corinthians 5:17 declares that God has made you a new creation. It is now time for you to take three steps down the path to living God's way.

Step one: Take time every day to read, study, meditate on, and apply the principles of Scripture to your life that you might learn to think and act like His child. The Holy Spirit will open your eyes to God's truth and will give you the grace and power to live for Him.

Before going on to steps two and three, take time to meditate on the words of King David, whom God described as "a man after His own heart" in 1 Samuel 13:14 and Acts 13:22. In Psalm 119:99, David claimed to have more understanding than his teachers. Was he bragging? Was his heart filled with pride? Not at all. A careful search of the Scripture shows that David had a heart that desired to do God's will, and it was obedience that gave him wisdom and understanding. Consider the following information gleaned from the verses of Psalm 119:

Verse 97: David loved God's words and thought of them throughout the day.

Verse 98: God made him wiser than his enemies because he did God's will.

Verse 99: David had more understanding than his teachers because he meditated on God's Word.

Verse 100: Obeying God's Word gave him more understanding than his elders.

Verse 101: He chose to reject the path of evil.

Verse 102: The Lord taught David, just as He teaches all who desire to do His will.

Verse 103: God's words were sweeter than honey to David.

Verse 104: David received understanding through the words of God, and therefore he hated the path to falsehood.

Verse 105: God's Word provided light to direct him on the right path and shown as a lamp for his every step.

It has often been said and is worth repeating, "If you want to know God's will for your life, get to know Him well." One thing is certain: God wants us to trust Him. Many years ago, when I was facing a turning point in my life, one of my students passed along this sage advice: "God's will for your life is what you would choose if you knew what He knows."

"Thus says the LORD: 'Let not the wise man boast in his wisdom, let not the mighty man boast in his might, let not the rich man boast in his riches, but let him who boasts boast in this, that he understands and knows me, that I am the LORD who practices steadfast love, justice, and righteousness in the earth. For in these things I delight,' declares the LORD" (Jeremiah 9:23–24 ESV).

"This Book of the Law shall not depart from your mouth, but you shall meditate in it day and night, that you may observe to do according to all that is written in it. For then you will make your way prosperous, and then you will have good success" (Joshua 1:8 KJV).

"In your relationships with one another, have the same mindset as Christ Jesus" (Philippians 2:5 NIV).

"I beseech you therefore, brethren, by the mercies of God, that you present your bodies a living sacrifice, holy, acceptable to God, which is your reasonable service. And do not be conformed to this world, but be transformed by the renewing of your mind, that you may prove what is that good and acceptable and perfect will of God" (Romans 12:1–2 NKJV).

"As obedient children, do not conform to the evil desires you had when you lived in ignorance. But just as he who called you is holy, so be holy in all you do" (1 Peter 1:14–15 NIV).

Step two: Tell someone what Christ has done in your life, for you are now a messenger of the good news that God wants spread throughout the world.

"Therefore if any man be in Christ, he is a new creature: old things are passed away; behold, all things are become new. And all things are of God, who hath reconciled us to himself by Jesus Christ, and hath given to us the ministry of reconciliation; To wit, that God was in Christ, reconciling the world unto himself, not imputing their trespasses unto them; and hath committed unto us the word of reconciliation. Now then we are ambassadors for Christ, as though God did beseech you by us: we pray you in Christ's stead, be ye reconciled to God" (2 Corinthians 5:17–20 KJV).

"Go ye therefore, and teach all nations, baptizing them in the name of the Father, and of the Son, and of the Holy Ghost:

Teaching them to observe all things whatsoever I have commanded you: and, lo, I am with you always, even unto the end of the world. Amen" (Matthew 28:19–20 KJV).

Step three: Receive Christian baptism (Acts 8:26–38), which identifies you with Christ, and join with a Bible-believing, Bible-teaching church. It will help your spiritual growth and is a place where you can learn to follow Christ's example by serving others as you join with believers to worship our Lord.

"And let us consider how we may spur one another on toward love and good deeds, not giving up meeting together, as some are in the habit of doing, but encouraging one another—and all the more as you see the Day approaching" (Hebrews 10:24–25 NIV).

"So Christ himself gave the apostles, the prophets, the evangelists, the pastors and teachers, to equip his people for works of service, so that the body of Christ may be built up until we all reach unity in the faith and in the knowledge of the Son of God and become mature, attaining to the whole measure of the fullness of Christ" (Ephesians 4:11–13 NIV).

"Those who accepted his message were baptized, and about three thousand were added to their number that day. They devoted themselves to the apostles' teaching and to fellowship, to the breaking of bread and to prayer" (Acts 2:41–42 NIV).

Final note: Make no mistake in your thinking about salvation. We, as sinful people, cannot be saved by anything we do. Isaiah 64:6 and Titus 3:5 make this quite clear. Jesus has done it all. However, if we have truly been saved by God's grace through faith in His Son, we will, due to our new nature, have a natural desire to obey and honor Him. Ephesians 2:8–10 tells us we are not saved by our works, nor do we keep our salvation by our works. Salvation is all the work of God's grace.

The famous eighteenth-century American theologian, Jonathan Edwards, expressed it this way: "You contribute nothing to your salvation except the sin that made it necessary."

But if we are true children of God, our works will demonstrate that we love Him. It's just like Jesus said: "If you love me, you will keep my commandments" (John 14:15 ESV). Earlier, He said, "If ye continue in my word, then are ye my disciples indeed" (John 8:31 KJV). The apostle John expressed it this way: "Now by this we know that we know Him, if we keep His commandments He who says, "I know Him," and does not keep His commandments, is a liar, and the truth is not in him. But whoever keeps His word, truly the love of God is perfected in him. By this we know that we are in Him. He who says he abides in Him ought himself also to walk just as He walked." (1 John 2:3-6 NKJV). The evidence of true discipleship is obedience to the teachings of Christ.

ENDNOTES

1   John S. Dickerson. *The Great Evangelical Recession.* Grand Rapids, MI: Baker Books, 2013, p. 98.

2   Ibid., p. 98.

3   Josh McDowell. *The Last Christian Generation.* Holiday, FL: Green Key Books, 2006, p. 13.

4   Leon Morris. *The New International Commentary on the New Testament. The Gospel According to John.* Grand Rapids, MI: Wm. B. Eerdmans Pub. Co., 1971, p. 361.

5   Emory H. Bancroft. *Christian Theology, Systematic and Biblical.* Grand Rapids, MI: Zondervan Pub. Co., 1976, p. 330.

ABOUT THE AUTHOR

Steve MacFarland has been an educator for forty-plus years, working primarily as an administrator and Bible teacher in Christian high schools; he has also served as an interim pastor and speaker in many Delaware Valley churches. He graduated from Bible college and seminary in Philadelphia, and he and his wife, Fran, have four children and fifteen grandchildren. Steve and Fran have been married fifty blessed years, and they presently reside in Mullica Hill, New Jersey.

Printed in the United States
By Bookmasters